D1084101

Taxation and Political Change in the Young Nation,
1781–1833

Taxation and Political Change in the Young Nation 1781–1833

DALL W. FORSYTHE

New York / Columbia University Press / 1977

The Andrew W. Mellon Foundation, through a special grant, has assisted the Press in publishing this volume.

LIBRARY OF CONGRESS CATALOGING IN PUBLICATION DATA

Forsythe, Dall W   1943–
Taxation and political change in the Young Nation,
1781–1833.

Bibliography: p.
Includes index.
1. Taxation—United States—History.   2. Tariff—
United States—History.   3. Revenue—United States—
History.   4. United States—Politics and government—
1783–1865.   I. Title.
HJ2368.F67   336.2'00973   77-822
ISBN 0-213-04192-6

COLUMBIA UNIVERSITY PRESS
NEW YORK   GUILDFORD, SURREY
COPYRIGHT © 1975, 1977 COLUMBIA UNIVERSITY PRESS
ALL RIGHTS RESERVED
PRINTED IN THE UNITED STATES OF AMERICA

To Ana Marie,
with love and gratitude

/ CONTENTS

/ PREFACE

IN THIS ESSAY, I describe and analyze the creation and adaptation of taxes and other financial policies in the early years of American history. Tax politics here is treated not simply as a topic of intrinsic interest, but also as a path to fresh insights about the processes of nation building and political change in the United States. We can study political change to build better theories to account for past patterns of transformation, or we can use such studies to search for more effective points of leverage to transform politics in the future. In either case, political change in America is a topic which deserves much more study by political scientists.

As my notes show, I owe a large debt to the talented and dedicated historians who have already written on many of the topics touched upon in this book. Without monographs by such scholars as Leland D. Baldwin, E. James Ferguson, William W. Freehling and Merrill Jensen, to name but a few, this essay would have taken decades to write. I hope other political scientists will put to use the rich treasure trove of data on the politics of the American past which has been laid up by generations of historians.

I have also accumulated a number of more personal intellectual debts. First, advice, support, and insight from James S. Young have been invaluable at every step in the writing of this essay. In recent revisions, I have also drawn heavily on work done jointly with Gerald Finch, who has generously permitted me to use some of our shared conclusions in this essay. Ira Katznelson, Theodore J. Lowi, and J. David Greenstone have also made suggestions which influenced the findings of this study.

The American Political Science Association awarded an earlier version of the essay the E. E. Schattschneider prize for the best dissertation of the year in American politics. I was, of course, grateful to the committee which made the award, and especially to Fred I. Greenstein, who took the time to make suggestions for improving the essay. At various times, Stuart Bruchey, Hebert A. Deane, Mark Kesselman, Frank Macchiarola, Jerry E. Mechling, Hugh O'Neill, T. J. Pempel, Richard Pious, Harvey Shapiro, Donna Shalala, Allan Silver, Ronald Stack, and John Tabori generously read some or all of early drafts and made helpful suggestions. Wallace S. Sayre also helped to formulate the original plan for research; had he lived to criticize the final work, I know it would have been much improved.

Also important was support from Russell Sage Foundation. An early draft of this essay was written while I was a Graduate Fellow there, and Hugh F. Cline and David A. Goslin were generous with advice and encouragement. Arlene Jacobs typed the manuscript with cheerful efficiency, and Joan McQuary at the Columbia University Press provided thoughtful editorial assistance.

Finally, the love and sufferance of my wife and my daughters have been indispensable. None of these many people can be blamed for the errors that remain here, but they can take much credit for whatever merit this essay has. To all of them, I offer my heartfelt gratitude.

Taxation and Political Change in the Young Nation,
1781–1833

1 / TAXATION AND REGIME CHANGE: AN INTRODUCTION

AT MANY MOMENTS in history, the imposition of new taxes has proved a severe test of state authority. Costly wars in Europe between 1740 and 1763 made additional taxes necessary in several countries. In France, resistance to those levies set the stage for the Revolution of 1789. In England, Parliament's attempt to tax the American colonies was the first link in a chain of events which culminated in the Revolutionary War. And in general, as Charles Tilly and his colleagues point out, the creation of a tax system—or, to use their term, expansion of a government's extractive capacity—was a central problem during the formation of national states in Western Europe.[1]

"Extraction" is an ugly but necessary term that neatly summarizes the complex strategies governments adopt to assure themselves adequate flows of revenues. Once so stated, it seems quite obvious that rulers cannot develop a central state apparatus without some degree of capacity to extract revenues from the subject population of a nation. Expansion of the national government's revenue system was a source of political controversy in the United States between 1781 and 1833, and disputes over new taxes during that period provide an excellent opportunity to examine the problems rulers face when they try to increase state capacity.

If government activity is limited by its revenue base, the extractive system is itself limited by a number of factors. For instance, the relationship between tax policies and a nation's economic base is complex and interactive, as both Ardant and Braun point out.[2] If a nation (or a backward region within a nation) lacks cash commerce and exchange, collection of tax payments in currency can be extraordinarily difficult, as the dispute over the whiskey excise suggests. At the same time, tax policies themselves can increase or retard economic growth, an effect acknowledged by both supporters and opponents of the protective tariff.

Equally interesting from the perspective of this essay is the link between a regime's extractive policies and its social control strategies. Discussing what he calls the "extraction-coercion cycle," Samuel Finer points out that expansion of a state's coercive machinery (to fight a war, for instance) imposes new burdens on its extractive system. Those burdens, when passed along to the subject population as added taxes, may provoke noncompliance and resistance, which in turn lead to further expansion of the regime's coercive apparatus—and so around the circle. Eventually, says Finer, this "extraction-coercion cycle" may be converted to an "extraction-persuasion cycle" by a charismatic leader, by new social welfare policies, by the domestic impact of war, or by some other intervening factor.[3] In the American examples set out in the next three chapters, disturbances in the international environment did indeed lead to additional revenue requests, and new taxes imposed without a war to justify them were often greeted by popular resistance, which in turn provoked the government to enforce its policies with coercion.

THE CONCEPT OF "REGIME"

Throughout this study, I will be using the time-honored summary concept of "regime," a term which I find somewhat less confusing than similar phrases now in regular use in political analysis. In its most basic sense, a regime is nothing more than the specifications of the constitutional order for a nation-state.[4] "Regime" is thus equivalent to the formal rules of political conduct as expressed in written constitutions, charters, or statutes, insofar as those rules in fact serve as practical working guides to acceptable political behavior. "Regime" also includes informal specifications of the political rules of the game, like the customs which govern political parties as they choose candidates for President of the United States. Even more generally, "regime" also specifies other important limits on political activity not usually included in ordinary American usage of the term "constitution," such as the major settlements defining participation in politics, the distribution of political benefits, the types and level of social control available for use by the political elite, the broad institutional relationships inside government, and even the legitimating rhetoric and language of politics. In this expanded sense, the term also includes what Mosca called "the political formulae" for a given system.[5]

For all but American readers, the word "constitution" might just as easily substitute for "regime." The British have no trouble understanding "constitution" in its broad sense, and English scholars discussing "the Stuart constitution" or the "eighteenth-century constitution" are not content simply to describe organization of offices or judicial findings of the legal limits of government power. They go on to discuss political struggles over state authority, taxation, or control of parliamentary districts and membership, and they use as sources not simply laws and court cases but diaries, newspapers, sermons, and letters.[6] But when Americans think of constitutions, they think of documents specifying the limits of government action, and when they think about constitutional politics, they look to the Supreme Court and to formal amendments to the United States Constitution. In this essay, "regime politics" is meant to suggest much more than that.

In their discussion of what they call "regime interests," J. David Greenstone and Paul Peterson suggest that most citizens value the existence of an established regime, if only because it provides predictable limits or boundaries for political behavior.[7] As David Easton has suggested:

> The alternative would be for the rules and aims of political interaction in a system to be largely random and indeterminate. In that event, members of the system would have to argue about day-to-day actions and decisions at the same time they questioned the fundamental assumptions about the way in which these daily differences should be settled. . . .[8]

The end product of a well-established regime is a relatively predictable political process, and a settled regime provides limits for the controlled conflict of "normal politics," those day-to-day transactions which occupy most political actors most of the time. Moreover, the shape of "normal politics," precisely because it reflects the political process under a given regime, can in turn serve as data for inferences about the character of that regime.

A number of other concepts in the vocabulary of political science are similar in their application or otherwise easily confused with "regime." Indeed, in ordinary language, people often speak of a "new regime" when a new President takes office in the United States or when a new Government is installed in Great Britain, confusing a regime with an administration or what Easton calls a set of authorities. Simply installing new incumbents in a system's political offices need not and, in systems with well-established regimes, does not lead to an alteration of regime. In 1969, when Lyndon Johnson retired to his ranch and Richard Nixon became President, no fundamental alteration of regime was implied. Indeed, it is a mark of the high level of regime institutionalization in the United States that most changes of administration do not presage changes of regime, and that few serious campaigns for political office are carried out with regime transformation as a major campaign plank.

It is also possible to confuse "regime" with "political culture," since both notions refer to rules of political conduct. As Sidney Verba defines it, the political culture of a society "consists of the system of empirical beliefs, expressive symbols, and values which defines the situation in which political action takes place." [9] But regime norms are fully operational, and serve as practical limits on day-to-day political activity. The beliefs and values subsumed in political culture need not be so limited:

> Political culture does not refer to the formal structures of political interaction: to governments, political parties, pressure groups, or cliques. Nor does it refer to the pattern of interaction among political actors—who speaks to whom, who influences whom, who votes for whom. As we use the term "political culture" it refers to the system of beliefs about patterns of political interaction and political institutions. It refers not to what is happening in the world of politics, but to what people believe about those happenings. [10]

In fact, it is possible to have a regime that operates in contravention to important values in the political culture. For instance, citizens may be taught to believe in equality as an important element in their political culture, yet the distribution of benefits under a regime may be far from egalitarian. But such a situation, while not uncommon, is relatively unstable, and it is to be expected that either regime norms or political culture will change to provide closer congruence between reality and belief.

Finally, it is possible to confuse "regime" with "political system." Many political scientists use "political system" to mean nothing more than "nation-state," although they intend at the same time to imply that politics within that unit is complex and interrelated. "Regime" is easily distinguishable from "political system" when used in that vague sense, since a nation-state can persist through several full-scale regime transformations, as the political history of the past century in France demonstrates.

Used more precisely, "political system" is sometimes meant to denote an interdependent set of political actors (groups or individuals) at one or another level of analysis. As J. David Singer explains it, this "system of entities" approach is obviously permissive in its definition, but "it insists that any system embrace and use as its units of analysis only individuals or groups, and not behaviors, interactions, roles, or relationships." Singer does not suggest that behavior be ignored. On the contrary, he argues that: "We must be interested in and attentive to not only the attributes of these systems and subsystems but their behavior, relationships and interactions. The difference between this formulation and that of the systems-analysis school is that we see these latter phenomena as *occurring within* social systems, rather than as *constituting such systems.*" [11]

The elements of a political system for purposes of this essay are the political elite, the subject-population, and the actors in the international state system. But a regime also specifies the most important patterns of interaction between those elements. To use a mechanistic analogy, the elements of a political system are very much like the major pieces of equipment—or "hardware"—that constitute a large computer complex, but a regime also includes the programming, especially the "deep" programming (in machine language) that prescribes the main modes of operation for the system.

Finally, many prominent social scientists, including Easton, Kaplan, and Parsons, use "political system" to refer to "systems of behavior." [12] As the discussion immediately above should indicate, this usage of "political system" is virtually indistinguishable from "regime" as it is employed here. But because "political system" means so much (or so little) to so many people, I use the term "regime" in hopes of avoiding some of that conceptual confusion.

POLITICAL CHANGE AND DEVELOPMENT IN AMERICA

If the subject matter of this essay is taxation, its goal is to deepen understanding of the process of political change and development in the United States. To achieve this goal, I must first demonstrate that change and development are in fact characteristic of American political history, and that conflicts over central features of the regime do occur. Such a task is not as easy as it might seem. In fact, one of the few propositions that unite radical critics and enthusiastic supporters of the American regime is their contention that the political status quo is stable, and change occurs only in small increments at the margins of existing policies.

Within the field of political science, I believe that the study of political change and development in the United States is inhibited by the overextension and oversimplification of a number of influential ideas first put forward by Louis Hartz. Hartz's own argument in *The Liberal Tradition in America* is rich and elaborate, but its complexities have sometimes been abandoned by his disciples. For instance, Hartz believed that because America was unencumbered by a feudal past, class conflict in the European mode was impossible, but he did not state that fundamental political or social conflicts *never* occurred in America. Hartz believed that American political thought rested on a firm consensual base of Lockean liberalism, but he did not therefore conclude that Americans *never* quarrel about essential features of the political order. Hartz believed that the American liberal language "does not understand the meaning of sovereign power," [13] but he did not thereby imply that central state power does not exist in America, or that the extension of state power has *never* provoked bitter battles. Finally, Hartz did celebrate American pragmatism in politics, stating that when ethics are taken for granted, "all problems emerge as problems of technique." [14] However, he did not therefore conclude that incremental adjustment of existing policies has been the only mode of political transformation in the United States.

The problems that arise from too facile an extension of Hartz's basic arguments can be seen in the conclusions about American politics presented by Samuel Huntington in *Political Order in Changing Societies.* Huntington suggests that the "static quality of the political system" in the United States is its most striking characteristic,[15] and concludes that its political structure can still be classified as an archaic Tudor polity. As he puts it:

The institutional framework established in 1787 has . . . changed remarkably little in 175 years. Political modernization in America has thus been strangely attenuated and incomplete. In institutional terms, the American polity has never been underdeveloped, but it has never been wholly modern. In an age of rationalized authority, centralized bureaucracy, and totalitarian dictatorship, the American political system remains a curious anachronism.[16]

Huntington's clear implication is that neither change nor development is characteristic of American politics. Students of aggregate voting behavior have proven the first half of that proposition wrong. As realigning elections demonstrate,[17] American politics does change, and it changes rapidly and discontinuously. But even so sophisticated an analyst of American political change as Walter Dean Burnham has agreed with the second facet of Huntington's argument. As Burnham himself puts it, "one of the most remarkable aspects of American politics is its non-developmental character."[18]

In Theodore Lowi's striking phrase, *"government is the only institution in society whose manifest purpose is to maintain conquest through the exertion of controls."* [19] In the United States, that conquest is still incomplete, as Lowi points out. But over the course of American history, the capacity of the central state apparatus to exert such control has increased markedly or, to use a convenient shorthand, political development has taken place in the United States. The design and testing of indicators for precise measurement of such development is difficult, but even the crudest measures of long-term growth in expenditures, tax revenues, and government employment show large increases in the capacity of the central government. James Young has stated that in 1802 the entire federal establishment—civilian and military—employed 9,237 people, or one out of every 1,914 Americans. In 1975, the federal government employed 4.995 million people, or one out of every 43 Americans. In 1802, the national budget was $7.8 million, or $1.40 for each resident of the United States. In 1975, the national budget was $324.6 billion, or about $1,520 for each American. A more useful indicator of state capacity is the percentage of gross national product represented by government expenditures. Estimates of GNP for the mid-nineteenth century suggest that the federal government's expenditures in 1873 represent about 2.6 percent of GNP; in 1975, federal expenditures accounted for 21.6 percent of GNP.[20] In short, the central state apparatus has substantially increased its capacity for control over the course of American history. Moreover, Gerald Finch and I have shown elsewhere that according to one measure of development (allocative capacity, measured by expenditures and revenues), such increases occur not in steady, small increments, but in sizable and discontinuous jumps, usually associated with disturbances in the international environment.[21]

The central purpose of this book, therefore, is to reestablish as a topic for serious study the linked issues of political change and political development in the United States. In the chapters which follow, I describe the development of a central component of the American regime, which is at the same time a crucial determinant of state capacity—its system for extracting revenues from the subject population. In several of the cases presented, members of the political elite will be observed consciously debating the impact and limits of the regime, and those cases can therefore provide useful data for generalizing about the patterns of politics which characterize such regime conflict. First, I describe the disputes between 1781 and 1790 over the broad outlines of an extractive system for the new regime in the United States. I next examine specific applications of those general policies through the imposition of, first, internal taxes, and second, tariff duties. In the closing chapters, I use these cases to generalize about patterns of political behavior and to comment on Theodore J. Lowi's influential policy taxonomy and discuss the question of regime components and variables more systematically, and suggest strategies for further research on political change and development in the United States.

2 / MONEY: THE "INDISPENSABLE INGREDIENT"

AS SEYMOUR MARTIN LIPSET and Merrill Jensen have pointed out, the United States in the late eighteenth century was indeed a "new nation." [1] With independence accomplished, America's political leaders had to establish their own indigenous regime, and one central problem of state-building in that turbulent period of early development was extractive policy. As Alexander Hamilton put it in *Federalist #30:* "Money is, with propriety, considered as the vital principle of the body politic, as that which sustains its life and motion and enables it to perform its most essential functions. A complete power, therefore, to procure a regular and adequate supply of revenue, as far as the resources of the community will permit, may be regarded as an indispensable ingredient in every constitution." [2]

Most of this chapter is a discussion of the battles to limit or expand that "complete power," as the rulers of the new nation debated the most appropriate way to assure their infant government a steady flow of revenues from taxes and loans. But this task was doubly complicated because many of the colonial disputes with Great Britain had centered on Parliament's power to tax, and those conflicts were not textbook history but rather first-hand experience for most Americans. One historian who has looked with care at fiscal politics under the Articles of Confederation believes that "nothing testified more to the audacity of the founding fathers than their demand that the people relinquish what they had fought the British to preserve"—the power to tax.[3] So a brief account of colonial debate over taxation is a necessary prelude to a more detailed discussion of the establishment of a financial framework after the Revolution.

THE COLONIAL BACKGROUND

Throughout the early part of the eighteenth century, a large body of legislative controls (called Navigation Acts) existed to regulate trade between Great Britain, her colonies, and the rest of the world. Within the colonies, no widespread opposition to these controls was evident, and the management of trade for the development of colonial economies and for the protection of British industry and commerce was an accepted state function.[4] Those Navigation Acts, even when they were cast in the form of tax legislation, were specifically designed for regulatory purposes, not to raise revenues from the colonies. To do that, the colonial governors had to ask the local legislatures to levy taxes, and those requests were often rebuffed.

Like most other European powers, Great Britain's financial resources were badly strained in the mid-eighteenth century. By 1764, the British government was heavily in debt after long years of war, and protests over heavy taxes at home were a threat to domestic peace. Under the direction of Lord Grenville, Chancellor of the Exchequer, the government turned to the colonies, whose defense had been so costly, to provide additional revenues. Parliament passed new customs legislation, commonly known as the Sugar Act. In its form, the new law resembled previous navigation acts, but its purpose was strikingly different. As its preamble explicitly noted, it was designed to raise money, not to regulate trade and, for that reason, the Sugar Act was, as Oliver Dickerson has put it, "a constitutional revision of the entire colonial system,"[5] designed to ease the tax burden of the English landed gentry and shift that burden to the colonies.

Americans were quick to note and to protest this unilateral transformation of the regime that governed them. The Massachusetts legislature complained, "we look upon those Duties as a tax, and which we humbly apprehend ought not to be laid without the Representatives of the People affected by them." [6] Other, more active, protests included the beginnings of a boycott of British imports.

Parliament nonetheless contined to tax the colonies, and in 1765 the Stamp Act was passed, which required the use of stamped (and therefore taxed) paper for legal and commercial transactions, newspapers, pamphlets, and playing cards. Although this tax was lighter than a similar one levied on British subjects at home, the protest from the colonists was swift and severe. Colonial merchants organized nonimportation agreements and boycotts of English goods. In several colonies, mobs rioted, pulling down houses of the gentlemen designated as collectors of the tax, destroying caches of stamped paper, and otherwise effectively blocking distribution of the paper. New organizations, such as the Sons of Liberty, sprang up; and nine colonies sent delegates to the Stamp Act Congress in New York, where petitions of grievance were dispatched to the king and to Parliament.

As Edmund Morgan suggests, those protests were clear statements of the colonial view of "the boundary of Parliament's authority in America. It could legislate, but it could not tax." The Stamp Act Congress put it as explicitly, if not so succinctly, when it asked: ". . . whether there be not a material Distinction in Reason and sound Policy, at least, between the necessary Exercise of Parliamentary Jurisdiction in general acts, for the Amendment of the Common Law and the Regulation of Trade and Commerce through the whole Empire, and the exercise of that Jurisdiction, by imposing Taxes on the Colonies." [7] Seeking to expand its extractive capacity, Parliament had inadvertently succeeded in provoking protest which threatened its authoritative control over the colonies.

At the time when Parliament was considering the American protests, Benjamin Franklin was in England, and he appeared before the House of Commons to offer a conciliatory explanation of the colonists' behavior which gave the impression that their demands were much less radical than they actually were. Franklin argued disingenuously that the Americans were not objecting to Parliament's authority to raise revenues, but were distressed at the imposition of internal taxes, implying that they would submit willingly to duties on trade. Moreover, British merchants, distressed by the effect of the Stamp Act on their commerce with the colonies, joined the Americans in opposing it and, in 1766, Parliament repealed the offensive legislation. Lest that repeal be construed as weakness in the face of mob action in the colonies, members of Parliament also found it necessary to reassert their authority over the colonies "in all cases whatsoever" by simultaneous passage of the Declaratory Act.[8]

Although some members of Parliament, including William Pitt, accepted the Americans' constitutional argument that Parliament had no authority to levy taxes without the consent of colonial representatives, the Ministry continued to seek revenues in the American colonies. In 1767, land taxes in England were cut and, to make up part of that deficit, Parliament took Franklin at his word and imposed heavy new import duties on the colonies. In addition to those taxes, the Townshend Acts, as the legislation was called, also established new, tougher enforcement machinery. Previously, taxes had been administered by remote control from England; now a board of customs commissioners was to collect these duties from its new headquarters in Boston, the center of disruption and opposition. Once again, colonial protest was strenuous, and commissioners eventually asked for troops to maintain order. Boston was governed under what amounted to military rule for nearly a year, and even as those troops were withdrawn, disruptive incidents like the Boston Massacre of 1770 were taking place. To enforce its new extractive levies, Parliament found it necessary to expand its coercive apparatus in the colonies, thus setting the stage for opposition to British rule on wider grounds than abuse of taxing authority.

Historians have argued persuasively that the economic burden of British taxes on the colonists was too light to account for the protest they engendered. Americans in the middle of the eighteenth century were quite prosperous. Taxes under the colonial assemblies were low, wages were high, and the cost of living was not burdensome. British subjects in the mother country paid much higher taxes—on the average, 25 shillings a year—than Americans, who paid out only about sixpence annually. Even though the new taxes and heavy fees, as well as a large measure of administrative harassment, were concentrated in a few trading colonies which were to become the center of the revolutionary movement, the economic impact of those measures still does not seem heavy enough to account for such radical resistance.[9]

Given the inadequacy of economic explanations, some historians argue instead that the colonists' opposition was idealistic, based on strong attachment to principle. For example, Esmond Wright has suggested that the Revolution ". . . was not caused by taxes—which the colonists could well afford to pay and most of which were in any case abandoned—but by the unwillingness of a number of colonial leaders to accept the principle of taxation by Parliament for any purpose about which they were not consulted." [10]

But struggle over a regime issue should not be dismissed as an empty dispute over "principle." From Parliament's perspective, the colonists were trying to shrink the "zone of indifference" within which government commands would be obeyed automatically; [11] if the colonists succeeded, the scope of Parliament's "institutionalized conquest" would be diminished. [12] From the colonists' perspective, Parliament had overstepped the unwritten provisions of the British regime which limited the government's authority to raise revenues; in the short run, the real economic burden of those new policies was small, but the potential costs were quite high. As Edmund Morgan states the issue: "If Parliament succeeded in collecting the stamp tax, there was no telling how much would be England's gain: every penny collected in America would be a penny saved to the constituents of the Parliament that levied the tax." [13]

David Ramsay, an eighteenth-century historian, argued that the British government's attempt to levy taxes in the colonies destroyed at one blow "the guards which the constitution had placed round property, and the fences, which the ancestors of both countries had erected against arbitrary power." [14] Moreover, the colonists were justifiably worried about the uses to which those new revenues might be put. They had come to expect that their tax money would support a civil list of British officials working in America but free from control by colonial assemblies, and that they would be paying to maintain an army to enforce unwelcome new taxes.

In summary, then, the Americans believed that British initiatives in taxation constituted substantial changes in regime boundaries—changes in the scope and legitimate objectives of state control which would lead to changes in the distribution of burdens and benefits under the political system. None of those changes seemed beneficial to them; in fact, all of them seemed designed to hurt them and help other groups in the system. Their initial protests were directed at preserving the preexisting regime boundaries but when it became clear that the British would not retreat, they substituted demands for a totally independent regime. And the struggle that ensued taught America's emerging political elite that questions of revenue were not to be dealt with lightly.

REVENUES UNDER THE ARTICLES OF CONFEDERATION

When independence was achieved, disagreements over the scope of tax-ing authority for the new central government remained, and the struggle over that question provides a clear example of the politics of regime defi-nition. From 1781 to 1787, a battle raged over the taxing power of the na-tional government involving sharp conflict between the Continental Congress and the state governments, mobilization of economic interests, and even hints of mutiny among the officers of the Continental Army. The attempt to expand the regime's extractive capacity by providing Congress with the power to levy its own taxes finally failed, and that failure was an important factor in the decision by part of the political elite to scrap the existing government and offer in its place a redesigned central state appa-ratus.

Because of their experience under British rule, the colonists were natu-rally wary of lodging much authority—especially taxing powers—in the national government they had created to fight the war against England. Under the Articles of Confederation, extractive capacity was severely lim-ited, and neither legal authority nor bureaucratic machinery existed to en-force the demands of the Continental Congress for revenues. Congress could not directly tax citizens or commerce, but instead could only ask state governments, through requisitions, to provide it with the funds it required. When the states were slow in paying their share, as was often the case, Congress had no coercive power to compel compliance, but was limited to whatever persuasive techniques it could devise to convince the state legislatures. Most citizens felt that:

> . . . under the Articles of Confederation the states remained in a position to check arbitrary proceedings by withholding revenue from the Congress—just as the states' own citizens could similarly curb the states' power. Agreement on this principle was so nearly universal that although proponents of strong government took part in drafting the Articles of Confederation, they never proposed that Congress should be given authority to collect taxes.[15]

In spite of these stringent limits on its fiscal powers, the national govern-ment was able to finance the war through emissions of paper money, through generous foreign loans from Great Britain's enemies in Europe, and through the financial wizardry of Robert Morris, a Philadelphia merchant who used his cunning and his own large fortune to keep the government operating for a number of years.

Morris was appointed Superintendent of Finance, but he and his allies were not satisfied with the revenue powers of Congress, just as they were not satisfied with the powers of the national government as a whole. As a first step, Morris made some patchwork suggestions for local initiatives which would improve the extractive systems of a few key states, and thereby increase their capacity to meet their requisitions.

In 1782, for example, Morris appointed Alexander Hamilton to the post of receiver of taxes for the state of New York. In that position, Hamilton proposed a full-scale revision of the state's tax structure, and recommended a set of new taxes remarkably like those he was to recommend for the national government as Secretary of Treasury a decade later. But the New York legislature was hardly anxious to tax its citizens more heavily on behalf of Congress, and showed little enthusiasm for Hamilton's plan.

In fact, over the long run, Morris and his nationalist comrades were less interested in making the requisition system work than in demonstrating its inadequacy and encouraging its replacement by direct taxing powers for Congress. Thus, they did little to make compliance easier for the states. In 1781, at Morris' insistence, Congress refused to accept either supplies or the states' own currencies in payment for congressional requisitions, nor were states permitted credit for their direct payments to the troops. Instead, the state governments were asked to pay out what was then the huge sum of $8 million in specie (in coined money, that is) or in the closest paper equivalent of hard money, Morris' own Financier's notes. Obviously, this initiative did nothing to smooth the requisition process, but instead made it even less likely that the states would comply promptly and completely.

Such activities exacerbated the inadequacies of the requisition system and, with his nationalist faction now in firm control of Congress, Morris and his allies moved boldly to expand the extractive capacity of the central government. James Duane, a nationalist member of Congress, indicated in a letter to George Washington how crucial independent taxing authority was to their scheme for reorganization within the framework of the Articles of Confederation:

> There are some political regulations . . . I have exceedingly at heart and which are now drawn near to a conclusion . . . the principal measures to which I allude are the establishment of executive or min-

isters in the departments of finance, war, the marine and foreign affairs,* the accomplishment of the Confederation: and procuring to Congress an augmentation of power and permanent revenues for carrying on the war.[16]

Specifically, as part of the "groundwork for the establishment of a national government," [17] the nationalists decided to push for a 5 percent impost—or import duty—on all foreign goods. This new taxing authority was to be coextensive with the existence of the national debt, and revenues collected from it were to be applied to payments on interest and principal of those war obligations. Although no collection procedures were specified, Ferguson points out that this expanded capacity implied a new enforcement apparatus, and that the "subsequent history of the impost leaves no doubt that collection was to be by federal officers." [18] For instance, even without the grant of the impost, Morris had moved in 1782 to establish his own staff of tax receivers (including Hamilton) in the states.

The impost of 1781 was quickly adopted by Congress as an amendment to the Articles of Confederation, and was submitted to the states for ratification in February of that year. (In fact, Congress passed the revenue amendment even before the Articles themselves were finally ratified in March 1781.) Immediately, another apparent weakness of that compact was exposed. For an amendment to be accepted, every one of the thirteen states had to ratify it.

In his arguments on behalf of the measure, Morris had pointed to the need for revenues to conduct the war and to assure that creditors would be willing to make loans to the young nation. To some extent, however, he undercut his own contention that loans would be hard to come by without independent revenues for Congress by his extraordinary success in negotiating foreign loans. Even more troublesome was the fast-approaching end of the war, which would undermine military justifications for the impost. Morris made bold to declare that, as a patriot, he would prefer that the war continue until the government was strengthened and national taxes established.[19]

But by the middle of 1782, peace was clearly close at hand, and Morris was forced to find new ways to justify his tax scheme to the public. Instead of emphasizing the necessity of the impost as a war measure, he

* The opponents of the nationalists, the old revolutionary group, preferred to see departments managed by committees rather than by single executives.

began to argue for it as a fund to discharge the sacred obligations of the Revolutionary debt, which was owed to widows, orphans, veterans, and other patriots. Since most of that debt had resulted from the operations of the Continental Army, Morris argued that its repayment was the duty of Congress, not of the states. Because of that national obligation, implying a contract between the public creditors and Congress which could not be valid without an independent source of revenue for the government, "the existence of the public debt implied a federal power of taxation," and was the only plausible rationalization for enlarged powers still available to Morris.[20]

Public justifications aside, the nationalists were well aware of some of the more practical implications of the debt. They knew, for example, how valuable the existence of a funded debt and a national bank had been in stabilizing the regime in Great Britain after the Revolution of 1689, where the debt had served to attract support to the government from important groups, most especially the monied interests. Writing to the Financier in 1781, Hamilton stated that "a national debt, if it is not excessive, will be to us a national blessing. It will be a powerful cement of our Union."[21] The nationalist faction obviously saw the debt as the key to marshaling public creditors behind their goals of increased powers for the central government. In November 1781, Morris wrote to Benjamin Franklin that it was his "well-grounded expectation that the clamors of the public creditors would induce the States to adopt the impost."[22] By discontinuing interest payments on loan certificates and at the same time proposing that future payments be contingent on establishment of federal taxes, the Financier made certain that those clamors would be loud ones. When he was visited by anxious delegations of public creditors, Morris suggested that they form organizations to press their views on Congress and the state legislatures; several such interest groups were soon active in the fight for the impost. Morris himself also wrote directly to recalcitrant state legislatures and governors, and his tax receivers lobbied in their states for ratification of the proposed tariff.[23]

At first, these sophisticated forays into pressure politics seemed to be succeeding. By the end of 1781, all the states but one had approved the impost amendment. In Rhode Island, however, the radical "country party" was still in power, and still firmly committed to limiting central authority. David Howell, Rhode Island's delegate to Congress, fought hard against the impost in the national legislature. After losing that fight, he went home to help his state legislature organize against the amendment. Merrill Jensen has summarized the debate in that state:

> Above all, argued Rhode Island, the impost was unconstitutional. The states would have no control over the income it would produce. The term of its duration was unlimited. Its collection would be an entering wedge for the central government to act directly on individuals, whereas by the confederation it could act only upon the states. This issue was thus clearly joined and recognized by most of the participants. The United States had a federal government. The nationalists wanted a national government.[24]

In short, the issue was not the nation's moral obligations to widows and children or the interests of creditors, but the expanding scope of control exercised by the national political regime in America, and it was so perceived by elite disputants in Congress and the state legislatures.

In a final attempt to secure ratification, Congress organized a delegation to travel to Rhode Island and argue the case for the tariff. But just as these envoys were setting out on their journey, they received word that the Virginia state legislature had withdrawn its approval of the amendment so quickly and quietly that even the governor of the state was at a loss to explain what had happened. With two states opposed, the impost of 1781 was dead, and the congressmen returned to Philadelphia.

Even with that discouraging failure fresh at hand, Morris was at work again by early 1783 to get Congress' approval of a new revenue amendment. Because the legislature was slow to act, he and Hamilton sought to open congressional proceedings to the public, so that members would be subject to the direct pressures of organized creditors. Morris also threatened to resign if Congress did not act on his proposals, and that threat was a serious one, since in times of financial crisis Morris had used his own fortune as well as his fiscal skills to keep the government solvent.[25] In a regime with such a fragile fiscal base, the resources of a single man could be crucial.

More ominous still, the capital began to hear rumors of serious discontent within the Continental Army, which was wintering at Newburgh, New York. The officers demanded back pay due them and, in January 1783, a three-man delegation arrived to present Congress with a strongly worded remonstrance threatening "fatal consequences" if their grievances were not dealt with quickly. Morris told them to expect very little satisfaction until national taxes were operative, and his associates talked darkly to congressmen about Cromwell's Roundheads, who had turned on Parliament when it tried to dismiss them without pay during the Puritan Revolution.[26]

Hamilton, who had been Washington's aide-de-camp during most of the war, delicately approached his former commander to determine whether he might be willing to use his troops—the central government's only coercive machinery—in support of the nationalist political program. First, he urged Washington to stay in position to be able to "guide the torrent and to bring order, perhaps even good, out of the confusion."[27] And then he made it clear what that good might be: ". . . the great *desideratum* . . . is the establishment of general funds, which alone can do justice to the creditors of the United States. . . . In this, the influence of the army, properly directed, may cooperate."[28]

In March 1783, only a month after Hamilton's letter to Washington, the crisis within the army was precipitated in what came to be known as the "Newburgh conspiracy." Officers circulated two addresses through the winter camp; one called a meeting without Washington's authorization, the other urged soldiers to stand firm and oppose disbandment until they had received their just due. To head off more serious trouble, Washington called his own official camp meeting, where he told his officers of his sympathy with their requests and asked them to remain moderate in their actions. Resolutions were passed which reminded Congress of the army's demands but affirmed its loyalty and, although some of the officers left the meeting in a rage, Washington had regained control. He rushed a record of the incident to Congress, and asked for immediate satisfaction of his men's demands.[29]

Only two days before news of the conspiracy reached Philadelphia, Morris had conveniently introduced a committee report recommending new revenue measures. By April, Congress had granted the officers five years' full pay in lieu of pensions at half pay for life.* Because that com-

---

* Although the officers were satisfied, the enlisted men were still troublesome. In May and June, Congress attempted to disband the army by "furloughing" the men with only one month's pay in cash and three in certificates. Some went home without a quarrel, but those stationed near Philadelphia mutinied and seized the city, threatening Congress and the Pennsylvania authorities, who refused to call out the militia to protect the national government. Members of Congress were forced to sneak out of their capital, and they spent several years wandering from city to city, "a government in search of a capital," as John Miller put it in *Hamilton*, p. 98.

mitment added substantially to the growing debt, the Congress also adopted another funding amendment for submission to the states. It included the 5 percent tariff, but added specific duties on salt, wines, rum, brandy, sugar, and tea. Moreover, the states together were to pledge payments to the central government of $1.5 million annually for twenty-five years. However, some concessions were offered as well. At the end of that period, the impost was to lapse, and during its tenure, its proceeds were to be applied only to interest and principal of the national debt. Moreover, Congress forswore any attempt to establish its own enforcement apparatus. The states would be empowered to appoint the revenue collectors, although Congress would retain authority to consent to the appointments and remove collectors when necessary.

Under strong pressure from the army and public creditors, all but three members of Congress voted for the measure. Opposed were the two radical members from Rhode Island and Alexander Hamilton, who objected to the twenty-five-year limit on the impost grant (because the debt would not be completely paid off within that period) and to the states' power to appoint collectors. In spite of his dissenting vote in Congress, Hamilton urged the New York state legislature to ratify the measure. Morris also initially opposed the amendment, which he felt was not strong enough. But Washington was now berating the nationalists for attempting to manipulate his officers, and the Financier, perhaps realizing that pressure politics could bring about no better outcome, withdrew his threat to resign and returned to work.[30]

Six states ratified the amendment quickly: New Jersey, Delaware, and Pennsylvania in 1783; South Carolina, North Carolina, and Connecticut in early 1784. After strenuous debate, the Massachusetts state legislature also accepted the proposal in 1783 and, at the same time, instructed its delegates to seek to abolish the office of Superintendent of Finance or to circumscribe its power. Virginia was badly split on the amendment. George Mason and the Lees opposed it outright. Thomas Jefferson and Patrick Henry disliked it, but supported its passage. In addition to their fear of a powerful Congress, Virginia's legislators were also disturbed because collections in their state would be large and their residents would pay more than their fair share of the national debt. The amendment was put aside in the first session of the legislature, but passed later in 1783.[31]

By 1786, the Secretary of the Congress reported mixed results in the struggle for ratification. Eight states had accepted the impost, but only three had agreed to pay their full share of the $1.5 million Congress had requested in supplementary funding. Several other states, including Rhode Island, had ratified the amendment, but their actions were technically unacceptable for one reason or another. Congress attempted to salvage something from the mess by asking the states to permit collection of the impost without full ratification of provisions for supplementary funding, but Pennsylvania refused this modification.

In New York a bitter fight was continuing. In coalition with large upstate landlords, delegates from New York City and the surrounding area supported the amendment, while the back-country farmers opposed it. The legislature finally agreed to the impost, but only if the state government was permitted to collect it. Congress found this condition unacceptable, and asked Governor Clinton to call a special session to review that action. Clinton refused and in the regular session in 1787 the legislature held fast to its position. Two days after the vote, "Hamilton moved the appointment of delegates to the Convention of 1787, and both houses shortly approved, moved in part no doubt by general alarm caused by Shays's Rebellion." [32]

In the Philadelphia Constitutional Convention, which was originally empowered only to revise and amend the Articles of Confederation, unanimity was no longer a requirement for action, and the nationalists finally won authority for the central government to tax citizens directly. Some of the delegates still wanted to restrict that taxing power, and the New Jersey plan proposed that the new government be limited to requisitions, import duties, and a stamp tax, although it was also to be granted greater powers to compel compliance from states who did not pay up their full shares. That was not good enough for the nationalists, who were anxious that there be no limitations on the kind of taxes the general government could levy. Eventually, they were almost entirely successful, and (except for export duties) no single tax was altogether denied the new Congress. However, the Constitution did specify that no direct tax could be apportioned among the states except on the basis of population. That prohibition had two plausible aims. First, as Charles Beard points out, it would help the rich avoid heavy taxes on their wealth: ". . . indirect taxes must be uniform, and these are to fall upon consumers. Direct taxes may be laid, but resort to this form of taxation is rendered practically impossible, save on extraordinary occasions by the provision that they must be apportioned according to population—so that numbers cannot transfer the burden to accumulated wealth." [33]

Contemporary observers indicated that the prohibition also seemed to benefit the southern and western sections of the country. In a letter to the governor of their state, North Carolina's two delegates to the Philadelphia Convention explained how the new constitution would avoid the "risque of unequal or heavy Taxation":

> It is provided in the 9th section of article the first that no capitation or direct Tax shall be laid except in proportion to the number of inhabitants, in which number five blacks are only counted as three. If a land tax is laid, we are to pay the same rate; for example, fifty citizens of North Carolina can be taxed no more for all their Lands than fifty Citizens in one of the Eastern States. This must be greatly in our favour, for as most of their farms are small and many of them live in Towns we certainly have, one with another land of twice the value that they possess. [34]

As later events demonstrated, Southerners were not so well-protected as they may have thought at the time of ratification.

Many nationalists were convinced by their experience in the Confederation government that they should vigorously resist the requisition system and any other restrictions on the power of the national government to tax. They also had strong positive reasons to support the central government's authority to collect its own revenues. They realized, for example, that the local governments began with a strong advantage over the new central government because, as Hamilton put it in a speech to the Convention, the states were the object of ". . . an habitual attachment of the people. The whole force of this tie is on the side of the State Govt. Its sovereignty is immediately before the eyes of the people: its protection is immediately enjoyed by them. From its hand distributive justice, and all those acts which familiarize and endear Govt. to a people, are dispensed to them. . . ." [35]

As Hamilton saw it, if the central government was to establish among the people an "habitual sense of obligation," [36] it must be free in every instance possible to act directly upon the citizenry, even in such matters as taxation. In *Federalist #27* he made the point elegantly:

. . . the more the operations of the national authority are inter-
mingled in the ordinary exercise of government, the more the citizens are accustomed to meet with it in the common occurrence of
their political life, the more it is familiarized to their sight and to the
feelings, the further it enters into those objects which touch the most
sensible chords and put into motion the most active springs of the
human heart, the greater will be the probability that it will conciliate
the respect and attachment of the community. Man is very much a
creature of habit. A thing that rarely strikes his senses will generally
have but a transient influence upon his mind. A government con-
tinually at a distance and out of sight can hardly be expected to interest the sensations of the people. The inference is that the authority of
the Union and the affections of the citizens towards it will be
strengthened, rather than weakened, by its extension to what are
called matters of internal concern; and that it have less occasion to
recur to force, in proportion to the familiarity and comprehen-
siveness of its agency.[37]

Moreover, Hamilton was anxious for the new government to establish
its own enforcement apparatus. As tax collector in 1782, Hamilton had
seen Morris' little corps of collectors lobbying for the impost, and he knew
the political value of a field staff. Indeed, under his guidance as Secretary
of the Treasury, the federal collectors (along with the marshals and their
deputies) became "the handy men of the federal administration," according to Leonard White, who catalogued their uses: liaison to the merchant,
fishing, and shipowning interests; advisers on local trends of opinion and
party maneuvers; and reporters on the qualifications of other prospective
appointees.[38] So Hamilton was forthright to his fellow delegates about the
value of a national collection staff and other federal patronage posts. As
Madison recorded it, Hamilton suggested to the Convention that ". . .
as the energy of the Federal Government was evidently short of the
degree necessary for pervading and uniting the States, it was expedient to
introduce the influence of officers deriving their emoluments from, and
consequently interested in supporting the power of, Congress." [39]
    In the debates at the Philadelphia Convention, taxation was of course
only one of several important issues, and delegates were more deeply
divided over problems such as the structure of representation for states of
different sizes, the character of the executive, and the role of the states in

the new regime. When the Constitution was submitted to the states for ratification, however, revenue issues assumed much greater importance, although they still were not the decisive question in any single state.

In the *Federalist,* eight of the eighty-five papers were devoted to Hamilton's discussion of taxing powers under the new Constitution. In them, he made two important predictions about the exercise of those powers which, on the basis of his later record as Secretary of the Treasury, seem disingenuous at best. First, he argued that the investiture of wide taxing powers in the central government did not mean that any sources of revenue (except import duties, as specifically stated in the document) would be denied to the states. Instead, those powers were to be exercised by both governments, each having "coequal and concurrent authority." [40] Roger Sherman and Oliver Ellsworth, delegates from Connecticut, had written their governor from the Constitutional Convention that: "It is probable that the principal branch of revenues will be duties on imports. What may be necessary to be raised by direct taxation is to be apportioned on the several states, according to the number of their inhabitants; and although Congress may raise the money on its own authority, if necessary, yet that authority need not be exercised, if each state will furnish its quota." [41] Hamilton was also reassuring about the rights of states, suggesting that ". . . the probability is that the United States will either wholly abstain from the objects preoccupied for local purposes, or will make use of the State officers and State regulations for collecting the additional imposition." [42]

Although Hamilton managed to calm those who feared double taxes and unnecessary revenue officers scurrying around the country, when he was Secretary of the Treasury he did in fact make special efforts to preempt large areas of taxation by moving into them before the states did. Nor did the structure of taxes allow for any significant independent role for the states at any time before the War of 1812.

Hamilton's second prediction was that the United States was likely to rely heavily on import duties for the bulk of its revenues and, as a corollary, that its power to gather revenues from other sources were not likely to be exercised except in emergencies. Excises were hopeless and "must be confined within a narrow compass. The genius of the people will ill brook the inquisitive and pre-emptory spirit of excise laws." Nor were direct taxes much better:

It is evident from the state of the country, from the habits of the people, from the experience we have had on the point itself that it is impracticable to raise any very considerable sums by direct taxation. Tax laws have in vain been multiplied; new methods to enforce the collection have in vain been tried; the public expectation has uniformly been disappointed, and the treasuries of the states have remained empty. . . .

Import duties were all that was left:

In so opulent a nation as that of Britain, where direct taxes from superior wealth must be much more tolerable, and from the vigor of the government, much more practicable than in America, far the greatest part of the national revenue is derived from taxes of the indirect kind. . . . Duties on imported articles form a large branch of this latter description.

In America, it is evident that we must a long time depend for the means of revenues chiefly on such duties. [43]

Hamilton later qualified his argument by pointing out that emergencies did arise, and other sources of revenues might be needed for meeting "the present and future exigencies of the Union," including the "two chief sources of expense in every government, . . . wars and rebellions." [44]

Hamilton's second prediction was reasonably accurate for the early years of the United States. During the first ten years of its history, the government collected $50.3 million (about 92 percent of its revenues) from duties on imports and from tonnage levies, while all other sources of revenue—including excises and other internal duties, postage, sale of public lands, and other miscellany—added up to just over $4 million. [45] Moreover, Hamilton's main excursion into internal taxation, the imposition of the whiskey excise, provoked more opposition than even his pessimistic assessments of "the genius of the people" might have led to expect.

Even after the ratification of the Constitution, the tax issue did not quite disappear. Wherever the Anti-Federalists had pockets of strength, they fought for their plan to restrict the new government to indirect taxes and supplementary requisitions, and every state that accompanied its ratification with suggested amendments included this proposal for limiting taxing powers. In the First Congress, that amendment was delayed in committee and, when it finally reached the floor, was beaten by a vote of

39 to 9. It was also ignored by James Madison, who served as floor manager for passage of the Bill of Rights. When the Congress enacted tariff legislation in its first session, the question was settled, and the national government was conceded the power to levy import duties for revenue purposes. But the struggle to define the new regime's extractive system had taken eight years to resolve, and was finally concluded only as part of a broader revision (initiated at the Philadelphia Convention) of all the elements of the national government.

HAMILTON'S FINANCIAL PLAN

The First Congress undertook a number of important financial actions, like the organization of the Treasury Department and the establishment of specific tariff and tonnage duties, which will be discussed more fully in a later chapter. But the most prolonged and bitter debate concerned Alexander Hamilton's grand design for the finances of the new nation, which called for full funding of the debt incurred by the Continental Congress, assumption of all state debts, the creation of a national bank, and the enactment of programs to assist manufactures. As one prominent economic historian has pointed out, assumption (and by implication the rest of Hamilton's package) was "the economic counterpart of the Constitution." [46] Hamilton himself, having worked so hard to expand the extractive capacity of the central government, was anxious to justify the full use of those powers. Moreover, many groups in the new nation were aware of the importance of the fundamental allocative issues at stake. They knew that as the government decided how it should deal with past commitments and how it should raise and spend its money, it would also be deciding who would bear costs and receive benefits under the newly organized regime, and they were therefore keenly interested in the outcome of that dispute.

Hamilton's blueprints for the cultural government's finances were presented in a series of "reports to the Congress from the Secretary of the Treasury." The first of these, the *Report on Public Credit*, sent to the legislature in January 1790, proposed full funding of interest and principal on the entire domestic debt of the United States at par (but with interest rates slightly below those promised by the Continental Congress) and assumption of all states' debts into the national debt. On the question of funding, Madison led a small but vociferous minority in Congress that argued that the national government should discriminate between holders of its debt. Those original recipients of certificates of indebtedness—Madison characterized them as widows, veterans, and patriots—should receive full payment; "speculators," who were any but those original holders, should receive only market value for their securities. Hamilton, who was surprised to find his former ally leading the opposition to his scheme, argued that such discimination was administratively unworkable and that it would damage his attempt to build confidence in the government's credit rating. The debate on funding in Congress reflected deep divisions in the country at large:

> Outside Congress, Madison's proposal brought to focus a residual hatred of merchants, rich men, and speculators which threatened faintly to give birth to a popular movement. Scores of newspaper articles denounced the present holders. They were said to have been loyalists or at least loyalists at heart, devoid of patriotism and given to exploiting the public distress. They were portrayed as following the soldiers to betray them with false information and buy their securities at a discount. Now that the fruits of national union were to be distributed, it was cause for bitter complaint that the wicked were to be rewarded and the virtuous made hewers of wood and drawers of water.[47]

In spite of a fair measure of popular support, Madison's forces in the House of Representatives were beaten nearly three to one. Discrimination was voted down, and the government was authorized to fund the entire debt at par, with interest rates of between 4 and 4.5 percent, depending on the conversion plan chosen by the debt holder. Although some of the speculators may have hoped for the full 6 percent promised by the Confederation government, they were well satisfied with the arrangements as passed, and the price of government securities was strong.

The proposal for assumption of state debts was opposed even more energetically. Altogether, debate on Hamilton's report went on in Congress from February to August 1790—almost all of the second session of the First Congress—and most of that time was devoted to discussion of assumption. Five times the proposal was defeated, each time by a slim margin.

For the most part, votes of members of Congress directly reflected the economic interests of their state governments. "Delegates from states that stood to lose from assumption were against it; those that hoped to gain were in favor of it; those from states whose interests were not greatly affected either way were indifferent." [48] Those perceptions of economic interest were in large part based on the amount of state debt remaining unpaid. Thus, delegates from Maryland, Georgia, and North Carolina, states with small debts, tended to vote against assumption. The delegation from Pennsylvania, a state with a moderate debt, was divided. New York and New Jersey had large debts, and those owed by Massachusetts and South Carolina were huge; their delegates supported Hamilton's plan. [49] Virginia also had a heavy debt, but its delegates were opposed to assumption because of a second salient economic consideration—the projections by the states of their status under the general settlement of the war accounts, which was then in progress. Virginia's leaders believed (incorrectly, as it turned out) that the national government owed the state a large sum for war expenses, and they expected that the settlement would extinguish its debt even without assumption. Some of the other Southern states also hoped to benefit from the general settlement, while some of the Northern states which would benefit most from assumption expected to owe the national government after settlement. The Southern states wanted early settlement, and were willing to countenance an indefinite delay in assumption. The Northern states were anxious to have their debts assumed, but were considering an attempt to delay settlement afterwards. [50] As a result, the Congress was sharply split along predominantly sectional lines, with all but one of the New England delegates favoring assumption, and most of the South against it.

For reasons which will be discussed below, assumption was a crucial part of Hamilton's overall plan for building a central state apparatus; so with the opposition in narrow control of Congress, he began to look for some acceptable compromise to preserve that element of the grand design. His bargaining chip was the location of the national capital. In 1790, the federal government was based in New York City, whose residents had just spent a substantial amount to build facilities for its operations and were understandably anxious to keep it there. Moreover, the merchants and commercial interests of New York enjoyed their proximity to the new state apparatus. Philadelphia, also a willing claimant, was the largest American city and had served as capital during the Confederation period. The South argued for a location along the Potomac, close to the geographical center of the Atlantic coast line. Hamilton met with Madison and with Jefferson, just back from Europe to assume his post of Secretary of State, and together they agreed that, after a ten-year stay in Philadelphia, a new national capital would be built in a federal district adjacent to Virginia and Maryland along the Potomac River. In addition to this important but symbolic concession, Hamilton also agreed to settlement procedures financially favorable to most Southern states. In return, two congressmen from Virginia (but not Madison himself) and two from Maryland agreed to vote for assumption, and the bill passed in the late summer of 1790.

With funding and assumption out of the way, the third key segment in the fiscal design was a national bank, patterned on the Bank of England. The second *Report on Public Credit* (submitted in December 1790) suggested that such a bank, jointly owned by government and private shareholders, could serve three essential functions: first, "the augmentation of the active or productive capital of a country," including provision of a stable circulating medium; second, "greater facility to the Government in obtaining pecuniary aids, especially in sudden emergencies"; and third, "the facilitating of the payment of taxes," especially by permitting loans to merchants who needed cash to pay taxes on schedule, and by increasing the quantity of money in circulation.[51]

> In contrast to the funding system and assumption of state debts, Hamilton's plan of a national bank made little stir outside of Congress. The country was prosperous; the Bank affected few individuals directly; and there was a strong prepossession in its favor among businessmen. As one of the opponents of the Bank said, "it was one of those sly and subtle movements which marched silently to its object: the vices of it were at first not palpable or obvious."[52]

The bill passed the House of Representatives in February 1791. Again the legislature divided along sharp sectional lines. Of the 39 favorable votes, 33 were from states north of the Potomac; of the 20 negative votes, 15 were cast by delegates from Virginia, the Carolinas, and Georgia.[53]

When the bill reached the desk of President Washington, a constitutional issue did develop, albeit one resolved entirely within the executive branch. Madison, Jefferson, and Edmund Randolph, the Attorney-General, sent the President memoranda arguing that on the basis of a strict reading of the Constitution, the bill should be vetoed. Washington initially agreed, but he did take the time to ask Hamilton for his rebuttal. In response, Hamilton wrote one of his best-known state papers, arguing for loose construction based on the "necessary and proper" clause of the

Constitution, an interpretation which later proved useful to many other political leaders concerned with the expansion of national power. Washington was convinced, the quiet debate ended, and the bill was signed.[54]

In December 1791, Hamilton submitted his famous *Report on Manufactures*. After a comprehensive survey of industrial facilities and capabilities of the young nation, Hamilton proposed a broad range of actions to promote manufacturing and to render America self-sufficient in such products as iron, nails, firearms, liquors, woolens, and cotton cloth. In addition to revisions of the tariff schedule in support of those ends, Hamilton also recommended direct premiums and bounties to developing industries, but the suggestions for such direct aids to business were largely ignored.

Hamilton's overall economic program worked toward three main goals. First, it was explicitly and overtly aimed at restoration of public credit for the government of the United States. In the debate over the proposals, it was this justification that Hamilton and his supporters pointed to time and again. An adequate extractive system must encompass not just tax revenues, but provisions for borrowing funds as well. Without repayment to those who had supported Congress with loans in the past, they said, the new government could not expect further credit in the future. In his first *Report on Public Credit*, Hamilton pointed to "these plain and undeniable truths."

> That exigencies are expected to occur, in the affairs of nations, in which there will be a necessity for borrowing.
> That loans in times of public danger, especially from foreign war, are found an indispensable resource, even to the wealthiest of them.
> And as on the one hand, the necessity for borrowing in particular emergencies cannot be doubted, so on the other, it is equally evident, that to be able to borrow upon *good terms*, it is essential that the credit of a nation should be well established.[55]

Along with the collective benefits of an improved defense capability, some other real benefits were forecast by Hamilton, including a lower interest rate, and an increase in value for landed property.[56] Hamilton's policies undoubtedly succeeded in restoring American credit and, by the end of 1794, the nation's credit rating was well-secured in Europe. Some government securities were selling at up to 10 percent above par, and foreign investment in government bonds had increased from $5.5 million in 1790 to $20.3 million in 1795 and to over $33 million in 1801.[57]

In addition to these relatively tangible grounds for its enactment, Hamilton also argued for his program on grounds "resting on the immutable principles of moral obligation." Not only was it recommended by "the strongest inducements of political expediency," he told his readers,

> . . . in proportion as the mind is disposed to contemplate, in the order of Providence, as intimate connection between public virtue and public happiness, will be its repugnancy to a violation of those principles.
>
> This reflection derives additional strength from the nature of the debt of the United States. It was the price of liberty. The faith of America has been repeatedly pledged for it, and with solemnities that give peculiar force to the obligation.[58]

His rhetoric must have had some effect. John Taylor of Caroline, one of the foremost exponents of agrarianism, later wrote a backhanded acknowledgment of the force of his opponent's arguments for "the public credit:"

> We moderns; we enlightened Americans; we who have abolished hierarchy and title; and we who are submitting to be taxed and enslaved by patronage and paper, without being deluded or terrified by the promise of heaven, the denunciation of hell, the penalties of the law, the brilliancy and generosity of nobility, or the pagentry and charity or superstition. A spell is put on our understandings by the words "public faith and national credit," which fascinates us into an opinion that fraud, corruption and oppression constitute national credit, and debt and slavery, public faith.[59]

Indeed, Taylor was noting the beginnings of a remarkable transformation of the nation's legitimating symbols. Although President Washington still rode in his coach-and-six and Vice-President Adams argued vigorously that the chief executive should be addressed as "His Elective Highness" and formally entitled "His Highmightiness the President of the United States and Protector of the Rights of the Same," * new grounds for legitimacy were being devised. In a brand-new nation, whose institutions had so recently been constructed before the very eyes of the public, compliance based on deference to traditional authority was at best tenuous. Hamilton and others were offering new symbols and arguments designed

---

* One member of Congress, unimpressed by the Federalists' aristocratic pretensions, decided that Adams should have his own title, and dubbed the pudgy Vice-President "His Rotundity." See Miller, *Federalist Era*, p. 9.

to elicit voluntary compliance without recourse to what Weber has called "the sanctity of immemorial traditions and the legitimacy of the status of those exercising authority under them." [60] That those efforts were in some part successful was demonstrated quickly enough. When Thomas Jefferson took office in 1801, he purged the presidency of all visible indications of rank, often riding along the Potomac around the new capital on his own horse and seating his dinner guests at a round table, so no status distinctions could be imputed. The prestige of the office of the presidency did not visibly decline.

The second goal of the Federalist fiscal system was to promote the development of the central state, and was not emphasized in public discussion. Hamilton wanted to weaken the state governments, which he saw as competitors with the national government for the affection and support of the citizenry. Although he had disavowed any attempt to preempt state taxes in his articles in the *Federalist,* Hamilton did in fact intend to establish national control over some sources of revenue the states might make use of in the future. In a discussion of the whiskey excise, for instance, Hamilton said that he "thought it well to lay hold of so valuable a resource of revenue before it was generally occupied by the State governments," and that he feared that failure to move quickly to put to use the new internal revenue power "might beget an impression that it was never to be exercised, and next, that it ought not to be exercised." [61] Earlier, President Washington had expressed his own long-range hopes quite openly in his first forecast of revenue sources, written before Hamilton joined his Cabinet. That paper contained his almost wistful suggestion that, given proper circumstances, including some direct federal payments to state governments, the states "will then have no occasion for taxes and consequently may abandon all the subjects of taxation to the Union." [62]

To rebuild national credit, which was the first goal of the Federalists, it was enough to fund the central government's foreign and domestic debt. But to undercut state revenue sources required that the national government have established and continuing uses for revenues large enough to justify those incursions. The very sizable debt that resulted from assumption of state liabilities was a perfect rationale for long-term taxation at a relatively high level, just as it had been the main justification for the nationalists in their fight a decade earlier for the impost. The fiscal requirements of that debt were indeed substantial. To service the national obligations of about $80 million (about $20 per person) required almost 80 percent of the annual expenditures of the federal government; and interest payments alone consumed over 40 percent of the national budget between 1790 and 1800.

Hamilton's third goal, equally intriguing from the point of view of this study, was to use these financial measures to cultivate some segment of the population that would concern itself with the survival of the new regime. As indicated earlier, Hamilton was well aware that the state governments commanded a wide base of support because of their extensive involvement in the day-to-day affairs of the citizenry. He also knew that that national government, whose operations fell "less immediately under the observation of the mass of the citizens," [63] could not expect similar loyalties to develop from habitual obligation and affective attachment for many years. Hamilton needed a quick answer to a crucial political problem: to whom could the new government turn for support, and on what terms was that support to be given?

In 1784, writing as "Phocion," Hamilton discussed a base for regime support unrelated to habit or affect:

> The safest reliance of every government is on men's interests. This is a principle of human nature, on which all political speculation, to be just, must be founded. Make it the interest of those citizens who, during the revolution, were opposed to us, to be friends of the new government, by affording them not only protection, but a participation in its privileges, and they will undoubtedly become its friends. [64]

Hamilton had watched carefully as Robert Morris used the national debt to draw creditors close to the new government organized under the Articles of Confederation. A decade later, the first Secretary of the Treasury realized that important sectors of the nation would benefit from his financial design; those beneficiaries were linked to the new regime by chains of self-interest, and Hamilton expected them to become its firmest supporters and defenders.

Debate over the Federalist program demonstrated the impact and effects of the extractive system on the nation's socioeconomic base. For that reason, the discussion also helped reveal some of the more salient political cleavages in the young nation, although conflict over the proposals were not always as expected. For example, although Hamilton's financial plan clearly favored the rich over the poor, debate over its provisions was not carried on along those class lines, to the surprise of Charles Beard, who noted that "one striking feature of this partisan conflict was the absence of any considerable appeal to the working classes or 'mechanics' in the towns." [65] Another historian offers an explanation:

> In some degree, this was a struggle between different kinds of aristo-crats. The planters of the South represented the old, established, land wealth of the country, whereas Hamilton's capitalists and specu-lators were to a large extent nouveaux riches. . . . It therefore struck Hamilton as highly ironical that southern planters should fulminate against "the privileged orders" quite as though they themselves were not conspicuous members of that order. [66]

Thus, in spite of whatever objective impact the proposed system might have had along the rich–poor cleavage, nowhere in "the varying shades of the conservative opinion which the new government represented" were advocates of the poor to be found. [67]

On the other hand, a closely related cleavage—between "those who are creditors, and those who are debtors," in Madison's words [68]—was both subjectively and objectively salient. Just as they had supported the pro-posals for independent sources of revenue for the Continental Congress, and just as they had supported the ratification of the Constitution, the creditors supported the Federalist funding plans, as Hamilton had ex-pected. Of course, his opponents argued that those who held the debt of the state and the national governments were simply speculators. And there is no question that speculation in government securities was ram-pant, with some traders going so far as to charter ships to reach Southern ports and securities markets before news from the North arrived to drive up prices. When Congress rejected Madison's proposal for discrimination favoring original holders, those speculators reaped a bounteous return on their gambles.

Another important economic division that was activated and irritated by the debate on the financial plan separated agrarian producers from other sectors of commerce and industry in the nation. Rural dwellers were by far the largest part of the population. Of the 4,009,000 counted in 1790, just 131,396 (or about 4 percent) lived in cities over 8,000 population, and only 201,655 lived in cities over 2,500. [69] When programs opposed by the agrarian population were enacted in spite of their majority status, resent-ment was inevitable. Writing in 1791, Thomas Jefferson was disturbed at what he regarded as the certain passage of the excise and bank bills: "The only corrective of what is corrupt in our present form of government will be the augmentation of the numbers in the lower house, so as to get more agricultural representation, which may put that interest above that of the stock-jobbers." [70] In that regard, the stirring speech of Congressman James Jackson of Georgia, an eloquent and impassioned opponent of the Federalist system, now seems almost touching in its disregard of the trends of the near future:

> We learn from Blackstone that the reason for establishing a national debt was . . . because it was seemed expedient to create a new interest, called the monied interest, in favor of the Prince of Orange, in opposition to the landed interest, which was supposed to be generally in favor of the King, who had abdicated the throne. I hope there is no such reason existing here; our Government I trust, is firmly established without the assistance of stock-jobbers. We ought to reign universally in the hearts of our fellow citizens, on account of the salutary tendancy of our measures to promote the general welfare, and not to depend upon the support of a party, who have no other cause to esteem us but because we realize their golden dreams of unlooked for success. [71]

Jackson realized that Hamilton was indeed looking to the "stock-jobbers" and "the monied interest" for support, and that the Federalist program did little to benefit his own agrarian constituency. As the history of Thomas Jefferson's own finances so tragically demonstrated, few planters—even the wealthy ones in the South—were creditors with cash available to buy government securities. On the contrary, they were usually heavily in debt to British or American merchants. They could not share in the profits made by speculators in the state and national debt and, instead of funding and assumption, would have preferred augmentation of fluid capital in the form of paper money issued by the states. [72] In addition, they could see that the Bank of the United States was obviously designed to assist merchants and manufacturers, not planters. In fact, in its charter was a provision forbidding the holding of land or buildings except under very restrictive conditions, and in practice the Bank refused to make commodity loans or to lend money on tobacco warehouse receipts. Finally, the very locale of its scope of operations was legally confined to places where there was "considerable Merchantile circulating Capital," thereby assuring it would be almost exclusively a nonagrarian resource. [73]

Of course, the funding system as a whole took in money from the entire nation through taxation, and returned it in large amounts—through interest payments of almost a million dollars every three months—to a relative few, making available funds for capitalist enterprise on a scale hitherto impossible. Once again, in disproportionately large numbers the beneficiaries of those transactions were located outside the agrarian sector. As one of Hamilton's biographers remarked, "with characteristic audacity, he undertook to run a farmers' republic for the immediate profit of businessmen." [74] The farmers knew that they were the losers in this exchange, and that the main winners were the merchants and the small but growing group of manufacturers. In this context, the famous *Report on Manufactures* can be seen in two ways: either as the promise of an immediate gift to the regime's new friends among the industrialists (Miller calls it the "dowry" bestowed on the fortunate marriage partner of the government),[75] or in a longer range strategy, as a device to broaden the Federalist party and state's support by increasing the number of people in the manufacturing sector, a natural ally of Hamilton's faction and an obvious candidate for growth.

The third important cleavage which became visible during the debate was geographical and was of considerable importance for the course of United States history during the nineteenth century. Without a doubt, the struggle over the Federalist financial system was an impetus to Southern sectionalism. The leaders of the South believed that their region was the prime victim in the fight; as Patrick Henry saw it, Hamilton seemed to be trying to establish the Southern states as "the milch cow out of whom the substance would be extracted." [76] Over four-fifths of the national debt was held by citizens living north of the Mason-Dixon line, so interest payments did not benefit the South as much as the North. For example, in 1795 Virginia, a state with almost twice the population of Massachusetts, received only a fifth as much in interest on securities of the United States.[77] Moreover, since most of the state debt was concentrated in the North, Southern states (with the important exception of South Carolina) benefited less from assumption than states in other sections of the country.

In his arguments on behalf of the Bank of the United States, Hamilton had indicated that he wanted the Bank's stock to "be generally diffused throughout the States," in order to build loyalty to the institution in all sections of the country. In response to a request by Madison, he also delayed the sale of bank scrip (which entitled holders to purchase stock) for three extra months in 1791 to give buyers from outside the Philadelphia area a better chance to attend the sale. But in spite of these good intentions and precautions, it quickly became apparent that the scrip and the stock were predominantly in the hands of citizens living north of the Potomac, and that those investors were turning quick and sizable profits on their holdings.[78] Once again, the government's public finance schemes profited the North far more than the South.

Hamilton said that the Federalist financial program was meant to provide collective benefits to the nation as a whole and to all of its citizens through the restoration of public credit. But his program was also the means for allocating particularistic costs and benefits to a number of regional and economic subgroups among the population. The debate touched upon important regime issues, especially the future exercise of taxing powers, the choice of beneficiaries of government policies, the allocation of the burden of providing revenues, and the sectors to which the new government would look for other sorts of support.

Because of the salience of those regime issues, the debates over the program included a rather careful accounting of the consequences of the measures. The clear beneficiaries were Northerners, and especially Northern state governments; creditors, and especially holders of state and national debt; and merchants and manufacturers. And these groups supported the program. Opponents of the measures were those complementary groups—debtors, Southerners, and farmers—who saw themselves agreeing to assume the burdens of the system through increased taxes, but could see no gains for themselves.

Conflict was intensified because there was a high degree of overlap along those cleavages—the South was more agrarian than the North, and Southern planters were generally debtors, while Northern merchants tended to be creditors. The beneficiaries of the policies realized that, in return for its favor, the government expected support from the Northern mercantile and financial elite: they were to lend it money; forswear smuggling and otherwise cooperate in the collection of taxes on commercial transactions; supply many of its officeholders; and in general defend the new regime against its opponents in Congress, in the press, and in the nation at large. In this important instance of conflict over regime definition, such were the costs and the obligations.

3 / INTERNAL TAXES

THE BROAD OUTLINES of the regime's extractive system were established in debates over the impost of 1781, over the taxing powers under the Constitution of 1787, and over Hamilton's plan for funding and assumption. As discussion turned to the specifics of taxation under that framework, an element of ambiguity in popular expectations about internal taxes became apparent. In the new Constitution, the nationalists had provided a full range of taxes for the central government, including excises and direct levies. But in their propaganda to promote ratification of the charter, they had also suggested that such taxes would not be used except in emergencies, and that the tariff would be the fiscal mainstay of the national government.

However, Alexander Hamilton's grand fiscal plan for the new regime was designed to justify immediate and generous exercise of the nation's revenue powers and, not incidentally, to build firm support for the regime among those who benefited from his policies. Thus, once in office, Hamilton moved quickly to propose internal taxes, using the large national debt as justification. The first case in this chapter examines the most controversial of those taxes, the whiskey excise. The imposition of the excise provoked opposition along the nation's frontier, and the central government met that challenge with coercion—a force of state militiamen under federal control. The next case deals with the second important component of the Federalist program of internal levies, the direct tax of 1798. In part because of a threat from the international environment, opposition was much less formidable, although Adams did use federal troops to quell a miniscule disturbance. The third case describes the enactment, in the midst of war with Great Britain, of a full panoply of internal taxes; no domestic protest was apparent.

THE WHISKEY EXCISE

Because the struggle over the Federalist financial plan was so bitter, it is not surprising to find groups on the losing side resisting taxes enacted to implement the grand design. Even without heavy new additions to the national debt, some federal taxes had been anticipated. The authors of the *Federalist* had indicated that import duties would be the main source of funds, and other participants in the Philadelphia Convention had so reported to their constituencies. Moreover, national tariff duties represented no real increase in the overall tax burden, since state governments, which had levied such taxes before the new Constitution took effect, were now prohibited from doing so. Finally, imposts were relatively invisible taxes, paid at the ports by merchants, and then quietly incorporated into the price of goods. For all those reasons, tariff duties were not initially resisted, as the next chapter will show. In fact, outside of the difficult strategy of boycotting imported goods, no effective resistance was possible without cooperation from the mercantile class, which was generally supportive of the new government.

But in 1790, in response to Hamilton's proposal that an excise on whiskey be enacted, Congress began to discuss internal taxes. Historically, excise taxes had been roundly disliked by the people called upon to pay them. In 1641, when a temporary excise was levied in England, riots broke out in London, the excise house was burned, and troops were needed to restore order. In 1734, another attempt was made to enact an excise, but the proposal was defeated in the House of Commons, and the students of Oxford took the opportunity to celebrate for three full days. During the American Revolution, the Continental Congress appealed to residents of Quebec for support in its Canada Address. One of its arguments was that the British have "subjected you to the imposition of Excise, the horror of all free states; thus wresting your property from you by the most odious of taxes, and laying open to insolent taxgatherers, houses, and scenes of domestic peace and comfort, and called the castles of English subjects in the books of their law." [1] And Samuel Johnson, in his famous *Dictionary of the English Language,* succinctly defined "excise" as "a hateful tax levied upon commodities." [2]

In the popular press, opponents of the Federalist proposal for a whiskey excise conjured up visions of excisemen prying into the affairs of citizens. Rehearsing themes from the debate on funding and assumption, the opposition also argued that the proceeds from the tax would be used to pay interest charges to wealthy speculators in state and national securities. In response, Hamilton and his Federalist supporters could justify this "hateful tax" only by pointing once again to the collective benefits the nation as a whole would reap from the restoration of public credit. The excise tax was inextricably tied to the rest of the Federalist financial design, and was intended to provide additional revenues for payment of interest and principal on the debt. In 1792, Hamilton pointed out in a report to Congress that import duties could not permanently meet that need:

> . . . as the growth of manufactures diminishes the quantum of duty on imports, the public revenues, ceasing to arise from the source, must be derived from articles which the national industry has substituted for those previously imported. If the Government cannot then resort to internal means for the additional supplies which the exigencies of every nation call for, it will be unable to perform its duty, or, even to preserve its existence. The community must be unprotected, and the social contract dissolved. . . . [3]

Hamilton argued that, relative to other manufacturing efforts, the domestic distilling business was a mature industry. Moreover, whiskey was not only a luxury, which for that reason alone deserved taxing, but was a danger to the moral fiber of the nation: "The consumption of ardent spirits particularly, no doubt very much on account of their cheapness, is carried on to an extreme, which is truly to be regretted, as well in regard to the health and the morals, as to the economy of the community." [4] So by taxing whiskey, which must be counted a "pernicious luxury," the national government was not only making a necessary contribution to the public credit, but was also regulating a morally destructive habit as well.

In Congress, potential opposition to the excise was undercut because

Jefferson and Madison had made a bargain with Hamilton on the issue of funding and assumption, and now felt that they had to support legislation to pay for it. From his position in the executive branch, Jefferson said nothing at all about the whiskey excise, and Madison told Congress that he could see no other way to raise necessary funds. So in January 1791, the House of Representatives passed the whiskey excise by a vote of 35 to 21. The South, including Maryland, opposed the bill; Pennsylvania and Virginia were evenly split; and New England, New Jersey, Delaware, and New York supported the legislation. Senate passage followed shortly.

The tax was designed to raise $800,000. Rates ranged from 7¢ to 18¢ a gallon, varying with proof, and were payable at the still head. In the same act, Congress created an internal revenue service to collect the tax. Each state was designated a tax district, under a supervisor, and was divided into surveys, with one or more inspectors. Surveys were often further subdivided into collectorships, administered by a collector who was actually to gather the taxes. Supervisors were paid a substantial salary of $1,000 and 0.5 percent of collections per year, inspectors $450 and 1 percent of collections, and collectors 4 percent of their receipts.[5]

Targets of this new initiative in extraction did not view the issue in the same terms as the legislators. First, most distillers did not see themselves as members of "a mature industry," or even as businessmen in any accepted sense of the word, but rather as frontier farmers operating their own or, more often, cooperative community stills of quite limited size. Nor were they convinced by moral justifications for the excise. Western farmers enjoyed their whiskey, but they used it for many purposes aside from drinking pleasure. It was a medicinal product, taken by women and men for almost any illness. More important, in a region with a primitive economic base, whiskey was an essential item of barter, taking the place of cash in many transactions. It was here that the excise hurt most. For even if the product was to be used only for barter, tax still had to be paid, since the tax was levied not on retail sales but on still capacity or production. Taxing the most available article of exchange caused real economic hardship in a region such as western Pennsylvania, where cash was so scarce that even ministers' salaries were sometimes paid in "old Monongahela rye."[6]

The impact of the excise was especially heavy in Pennsylvania's fourth survey, which lay in and around the frontier town of Pittsburgh—at that time, nearly one-fourth of all the stills in the entire United States were located in that area. Even the sturdy farmers of western Pennsylvania could not drink all that whiskey. Rather the liquor was a central item in the region's trade with the East. On the long trip over the mountains, a horse could carry four bushels of ground rye; if that grain was distilled into whiskey, the same animal could carry two eight-gallon kegs, the product of twenty-four bushels of rye. In the West, whiskey was cheap, selling for as little as 25¢ a gallon. Over the mountains, the same spirits might bring twice that, and although much of that extra price was absorbed by shipping costs, it was still much more profitable to ship whiskey East than to ship grain or sell whiskey on the frontier. Since the tax of about 8¢ a gallon represented a high percentage of the costs of whiskey, the excise was seen as threatening to this trade. Moreover, payment in cash was required, and a frontier farmer did not often see hard money.

Nor did the "whiskey boys" see how they benefited from the state activities supported by these duties. The Federalists had argued that the excise was necessary to assure the nation's credit so that it could borrow in times of international crisis, but no such crisis existed when the excise was enacted. Hamilton also tried to remind frontier residents of the dangers of Indian wars, and suggested that they might prefer the presence of a tax collector to hostile savages at their door.[7] But that justification was hardly overpowering; the westerners knew that the central government was three hundred miles distant, and that the burden of day-to-day defense against the Indians lay with their own militia companies.

In fact, encouraged by the arguments of their delegates during the debate in Congress, the residents of the frontier perceived the excise as an attempt to avoid land taxes which would have hit the East heavily, since its land was improved and close to markets, and consequently more valuable.[8] Nor was the frontier fooled by the presentation of the tax as a duty on a manufactured product. A congressman from North Carolina opposed the levy on distilling because:

> . . . it operates, and is in fact, a tax upon this occupation and agriculture, as they stand connected in one part of the union, while manufacturers in other parts are not only rewarded by high protecting duties, but in some instances even by specified bounties. The agricultural interest has experienced the most unfavorable influence of this law likewise, and it operates most oppressively too upon that class of farmers whose estates are situated in the interior country,

and whose interests have thus far passed almost unnoticed in the policy of the general government.[9]

In the words of one modern historian:

> What government had done was to tax one group of people (chiefly, buyers of imported goods and grain farmers who converted their crops into whiskey) for the immediate benefit of a smaller group of people (securities holders) in order to achieve a later and larger benefit for the American community as a whole.[10]

However, those distant collective benefits were small consolation for the immediate and relatively serious economic dislocation caused by high cash taxes on a prime circulating medium and export product, an article that in the West was regarded as "an indispensable necessity to life, health, and happiness." [11]

Between 1684 and 1791, the colony and state of Pennsylvania had levied its own excise on liquor, but before the Revolution little attempt was made to tax domestic products unless they were sold at retail. In 1780, Pennsylvania passed a more stringent tax to provide revenues for its share of Congress' requisitions for army pay, but collections were poor, totaling only about £15,000 a year. In the frontier sections of western Pennsylvania, the state's enforcement was almost a joke. When not subsisting on small bribes, collectors were subject to a wide variety of minor harassments.

When faced with the national government's early attempts to collect its new whiskey excise in 1791 and 1792, the frontiersmen reacted as they had for decades: they refused to pay and intimidated collectors with acts of limited violence—one revenue agent was tarred and feathered, for example. Congressman Sedgwick of Massachusetts had some cause to be pleased with his prescience. During the debate on assumption, he had predicted that Congress would have to levy excises to support the enlarged debt, and he warned that an attempt to collect them might lead to violence. Although he expected such resistance to arise in western Massachusetts, other frontier communities seemed to be validating his prophecy.[12]

Since part of Hamilton's purpose in proposing the excise had been to diminish the power of states, he must have expected the denunciations of the excise bill that came from the legislatures of Virginia, Maryland,

North Carolina, and Pennsylvania.[13] William Maclay, an energetic opponent of Hamilton in the Senate, also saw the issue in terms of its effects on
the local units:

> Annihilation of State government is undoubtedly the object of these
> people. . . . They have created an Indian war, that an army may
> spring out of it; and the trifling affairs of our having eleven captives at
> Algiers (who ought long ago to have been ransomed) is made the pre-
> text for going to war with them and fitting out a fleet. With these two
> engines, and the collateral aid derived from a host of revenue of-
> ficers, farewell freedom in America.[14]

These protests were predictable. More serious was the evidence of noncompliance and overt acts of opposition from the distillers in the West.
Hamilton's first response was to recommend small but conciliatory modifications in the law. In May 1792, the excise act was altered in favor of the
distillers, with tax rates reduced and payment schedules liberalized.[15]
Another important grievance on the frontier was the law's requirement
that excise cases be heard only in Federal district courts. For citizens of
western Pennsylvania, the nearest court was in Philadelphia, and an appearance there necessitated a trip of nearly three hundred miles, absence
from the farm for a number of weeks, and cash payments for lawyers and
witnesses. In March 1793, Congress authorized special sessions nearer the
scene of alleged offenses (although such trials were never held in the
fourth survey) and, in June 1794, Congress made excise cases cognizable
in state courts if they occurred more than fifty miles from a U.S. district
court.[16]

Hamilton had a remarkably analytic view of the tasks of nation-building
and he seemed well aware that, as Richard Merritt has put it, one of the
most important requirements of an amalgamated political community is
"the willingness of the members to comply with the demands of the common government, at least in most cases most of the time."[17] One way to
increase compliance was to make the demands less onerous, as the central
government had done by reducing the excise rates and changing court
procedures. But President Washington was not willing to travel too far
along the road to compromise. In his first annual address to Congress, he
had stated that Americans had to learn "to distinguish between oppression
and the necessary exercise of lawful authority,"[18] and Hamilton took his
mentor's admonition to heart. In 1792, the Secretary of the Treasury

complained that in North Carolina as well as the four western counties of Pennsylvania the excise "had never been in any degree submitted to," [19] and argued that if the government failed to act soon, it ran heavy risks:

> My present conviction is, that it is indispensable, if competent evidence can be obtained, to exert the full force of the law against the offenders, with every circumstance that can manifest the determination of government to enforce its execution; and if the processes of the court are resisted, as is rather to be expected, to employ those means which in the last resort are in the power of the Executive. If this is not done, the spirit of disobedience will naturally extend, and the authority of the government will be prostrated. Moderation enough has been shown; it is time to assume a different tone. The well-disposed part of the community will begin to think the Executive wanting in decision and vigor. [20]

Two weeks later, Washington issued a stern public proclamation admonishing the tax offenders and threatening severe action in the future. But apart from that statement, the government undertook no serious enforcement efforts during the next eighteen months.

In May 1794, Tench Coxe, one of Hamilton's assistants in the Treasury Department, announced his inability to enforce the excise law in Kentucky and the western part of South Carolina, and further reported that the law was so widely ignored in Pennsylvania that the supervisor for the state had been unable to make any report for two years. [21] It was in the latter state, where most of the stills were located and where disobedience was most flagrant, that the government chose to act. That action precipitated widespread and overt resistance to the law and to the government that sought to enforce it.

As indicated above, Congress had modified the requirement that all cases under the excise law be heard in U.S. district courts, and had made it possible for violations occurring more than fifty miles from such a court to be heard before state judges. However, a week before that concession was to take effect in June 1794, writs were entered in the federal court in Philadelphia against unregistered distillers in western Pennsylvania's fourth survey. In July, when frontier distillers assumed they were finally immune from such action, federal officials began to serve processes requiring appearances in Philadelphia.

Although there is no direct evidence that this action was undertaken at

Hamilton's instigation, his enemies gave him credit for it, and interpreted it as an attempt to provoke a violent crisis. Hamilton justified the move by arguing that the government had "no choice but to try the efficacy of the laws in prosecuting with vigor delinquents and defendants," and that it was unfair to those who had complied with the law and paid their taxes to let those who had disobeyed escape unpunished.[22] Leland Baldwin, the foremost historian of the Whiskey Rebellion, saw political motivations in the act, and pointed to Hamilton as the culprit:

> "It is difficult to escape the suspicion that the headstrong leader of the Federalists saw a heavensent opportunity to strengthen his regime by proving the necessity of a standing army and at the same time bring into disrepute the windy Democratic societies of the East by attacking their weaker western brethren who had been incautious enough to commit overt acts against the law." [23]

In any event, the summonses did provoke open and militant resistance in the West, where citizens moved with finality beyond simple and relatively passive noncompliance. For example, radicals began to revive the custom so prevalent during the Revolution of erecting liberty poles, which were understood to signify a call for popular uprising against government tyranny. The poles bore streamers and inscriptions, such as "An equal tax, and no excise. No asylum for traitors and cowards." Some of them even bore six-striped flags, an implicit demand that the six western counties in the area form a separate political unit.[24]

Such symbolic protests, while alarming to supporters of the young regime, were only a small step toward rebellion, and some contemporary observers argued that the "whiskey boys" never did take any further steps. In 1795, Thomas Jefferson said of the Whiskey Rebellion that "an insurrection was announced and proclaimed and armed against, but could never be found." [25] However, a number of overt acts made it clear that the government did have some basis for concern and action. As mentioned earlier, federal collectors had already been tarred and feathered in western Pennsylvania. During the summer of 1794, moreover, a mob of about 500 men, many of them members of the state militia, attacked the house of the federal inspector for that survey, who had just attempted to serve summonses on recalcitrant distillers. Some of the attackers died in the assault, and the house and its furnishings were destroyed. Memories of mob action during the Stamp Act crisis must have stirred in many a national official.

In other incidents in 1794, barns were burned, and federal revenue collectors forced to resign under threat of physical harm, as the king's distributors of stamped paper had once surrendered their posts under pressure from New Englanders. The whiskey rebels also robbed the U.S. mail outside of Pittsburgh. Most impressive of all, in late July and early August, they gathered together somewhere between 1,500 and 5,000 men (observers' counts differ) in milita companies to discuss further action. The meeting was held in Braddocks Field, in plain sight of Pittsburgh. Many of that town's officials and leading citizens had opposed the excise protests, and some of the angry rebels urged that the tiny city be burned.[26]

As if the problems in Pennsylvania were not sufficiently threatening, federal officials were also receiving news of sympathetic riots elsewhere during the summer of 1794. Virginia was full of troubles. A collector in Ohio County was attacked and his papers were stolen. In Monongalia County, another revenue official was forced to resign in a near riot. Groves of liberty poles sprang up in Winchester and Martinsburg, and the militia had to be summoned to quell one incident. In central Pennsylvania and Maryland, there were other riots, and insurgents took an arsenal and controlled a small town for several days. (Some of these events occurred in September, and probably were not caused so much by sympathy with the "whiskey rebels" as by opposition to draft calls to raise an army to quiet the rebellion in the West.)[27]

By late July, the situation was so serious that the Democratic Society in Philadelphia, in spite of its unrelenting hostility to Hamilton and his internal revenue polices, felt compelled to make a public disclaimer: "Although we conceive Excise systems to be oppressively hostile to the liberties of this country and a nursery of vice and sycophancy, we, notwithstanding, highly disapprove of every opposition to them, not warranted by that frame of government which has received the sanction of the people of the United States."[28] Legitimate opposition had escalated into noncompliance and resistance to the regime, and the political men of the young Republican party wanted no part of it. Their goal was capture of the central state apparatus, not its destruction.

Faced with this open challenge, the national government responded with coercion—or, as Hamilton had more delicately put it, with "those means which in the last resort are in the power of the Executive." On August 2, top federal officials met with the leadership of the state of Pennsylvania. Although state officials suggested additional court proceedings,

Hamilton and Washington reminded them that the house of a federal official had been burned, and emphasized their resolve to send troops. On August 4, U.S. Justice James Wilson issued the necessary certification, affirming that enforcement of the laws in western Pennsylvania was being "obstructed by combinations too powerful to be suppressed" by judicial processes. Three days later, Washington issued a proclamation demanding that the obstruction be ended, and on the same day issued orders to the governors of Pennsylvania, New Jersey, Maryland, and Virginia to call out 13,000 militiamen. In conjunction with the Pennsylvania governor, Washington also appointed a delegation of commissioners to investigate and negotiate with the rebels. During that same busy week, Hamilton wrote up an official report on the history of the occurrences thus far, which he followed with a more partisan defense of the government's action to be printed in the newspapers under the pseudonym, "An American." [29] Most citizens seemed far less enthusiastic than Hamilton about the application of coercion to enforce the excise. As mentioned earlier, there was opposition to draft calls in the states, especially in central Pennsylvania where Governor Mifflin had to personally undertake a speaking tour to exhort citizens to fill the troop quotas. But Hamilton was convinced that a large force of men was necessary. Five years later, in a note of advice to another cabinet member dealing with what appeared to be a minor uprising, the retired Secretary of the Treasury cautioned him: "Beware, my dear sir, of magnifying a riot into an insurrection, by employing in the first instance an inadequate force. 'Tis far better to err on the other side. Whenever the government appears in arms, it ought to appear like a *Hercules*, and inspire respect by the display of Strength. The consideration of expense is of no moment compared with the advantages of energy." [30]

The decision to use militia in place of the regular army was not unexpected, but it did have strategic overtones, since it was the choice which national officials hoped would arouse the least antagonism from the public. By using state forces instead of a unit of the small federal army (who in any case were badly stationed for an expedition on the Pennsylvania frontier), Hamilton and Washington hoped to quiet the "fashionable language" and rumors related by Madison that the insurrection would "establish the principle that a standing army was necessary for *enforcing the laws*." [31] Washington had long ago anticipated such complaints if regular troops were to be used. As early as 1792, as he thought about what action might be needed to enforce his first proclamation on the excise resistance, he wrote to Hamilton:

> And here not only the constitution and the laws must strictly govern, but the employing of the regular troops avoided, if it be possible to effect order without their aid; otherwise there will be a cry at once, "The cat is let out; we now see for what purpose an army was raised." Yet, if no other means will effectually answer, and the constitution and the laws will authorize these, they must be used as the dernier resort.[32]

As the militia companies were being gathered, Washington spent three very visible weeks in the field reviewing his troops in Maryland and Pennsylvania. Just before they set out to cross the mountains, he turned back. Hamilton rode on west and seemed to make most of the important decisions, although the forces were under the nominal control of Governor Henry Lee of Virginia.[33]

Even before the troops had left their base camps, the federal commissioners were in the fourth survey, collecting information and seeking peaceful means to end the conflict. After negotiation with the rebel leadership, they agreed to grant amnesty in exchange for individuals' declarations of submission to the United States during a referendum. But the referendum on September 11 was badly organized and poorly attended. Oaths of allegiance were not available for signing, and the radicals harassed citizens coming to the polls. The commissioners reported that they thought a majority of the citizens were willing to submit to the law, but that they were intimidated by a violent minority. In their report to the President, they saw no possibility of enforcing the law without extrajudicial assistance, and called for an acceleration of military preparations.[34]

In a final attempt to avoid direct military intervention, a meeting of frontier citizens and their "steering committee" was called at Parkinson's Ferry on October 2. In that conclave, the radicals were an outvoted minority, and resolutions were passed promising submission and testifying to the "general disposition" of the community to obey all laws. To convince federal officials to hold back the troops, the assembly appointed a delegation to travel east. That group did meet with Washington and Hamilton, but were unable to persuade them to turn back.[35]

The army arrived in the area, arrested a small number of prominent rebels, and started home on November 19, only three weeks after its coming. Fifteen hundred militiamen remained until spring, coexisting uneasily with the townspeople, who were displeased by the presence of an occupation force. Of one group of twenty prisoners who were taken to Philadelphia for trial, none was convicted. In another group, two were finally found guilty, but were pardoned by the President.[36] The insurrection was over, overt resistance was ended, the military expedition was a success, and taxes were being collected. Hamilton had succeeded in establishing an adequate level of compliance to his government's commands.

However, receipts from the excise did not turn out to be an important source of revenues for the government, and their cost of collection was very high when compared with the internal taxes levied two decades later during the War of 1812. Shortly after Jefferson took office in 1801, he and Albert Gallatin, his new Secretary of the Treasury, decided on their own long-range financial program. It included rapid repayment and retirement of the national debt, abolition of internal taxes, and severe cuts in expenditures to help reconcile the other two conflicting goals. At first, Jefferson and Gallatin disagreed about the feasibility of immediate tax reductions. Gallatin believed that repeal of internal duties should take second place to the administration's primary fiscal objective, debt reduction.[37] Jefferson insisted on abolition of internal taxes and Gallatin eventually agreed, but compensated by cutting expenditures even more heavily than originally planned. When John Randolph, chairman of the House Ways and Means Committee, submitted the legislation to repeal the excise tax, he also "introduced a bill to bring about Gallatin's dearest wish—an annual appropriation of $7,300,000 towards payment of the principal and interest of the public debt." [38]

Alexander Hamilton objected strongly to the destruction of his revenue system. In newspaper articles under the signature of "Lucius Crassus," he argued that without internal taxes the nation would be inadequately prepared in case of war or other sudden exigency, since import duties (the sole remaining source of revenues) were peculiarly subject to changes in international trade flows that arise during emergencies. According to Hamilton, Jefferson believed that, "Good patriots must at all events please the people," and was acting irresponsibily to gain popularity for himself and his party.[39]

But Hamilton's attempt to stir up opposition to repeal was unsuccessful.

The Federalists in Congress did suggest that it might be better to offer tax relief on necessities burdened by import duties such as salt, sugar, tea, and coffee, rather than on whiskey, but they made no serious attempt to block the tax reductions, and repeal sailed smoothly through both the House and the Senate. Needless to say, no objections from the citizenry were heard when the taxes were abolished. Hamilton's attempt to install internal taxes as a permanent feature of the American political regime had been roundly defeated.

THE DIRECT TAX OF 1798

In addition to tariffs and excises, the Constitution permitted the national government to tax people or property directly, so long as those taxes were apportioned according to population. As indicated in chapter 2, Hamilton was aware that direct taxes, like all internal duties, were unpopular. But he was anxious to exercise all the revenue powers available to the new government, and he had long known the value of crisis in uniting a country. As far back as 1781, in writing to Robert Morris about new taxes for the national government, Hamilton asserted that "the object of the war . . . would supply the want of habit, and reconcile the minds of the people to paying to the utmost of their ability," even in a brand-new country like America, "where the people have been so little accustomed to taxes." [40] Later he pointed out in his *Report on Manufactures* that direct taxes were "apt to be oppressive to different parts of the community, and, among other ill effects, have a very unfriendly aspect towards manufactures." But he was nonetheless prepared to use them in "cases of distressing emergency," [41] when presumably they might be better tolerated.

As early as 1794, a special committee of the House of Representatives on the public credit had suggested stamp duties and a direct tax to yield $750,000. Both recommendations were temporarily shelved. In 1797, French harassment of American shipping was stepped up as a tactic in the war with Great Britain. At the same time, the American envoy to France was expelled and instructed to inform his government that no new representative would be welcome until French demands regarding American trade with England were met. John Adams, in a presidential message to a special session of Congress in May 1797, proposed to send a new delegation in hopes that France would resume diplomatic relations. But at the same time, he suggested that the nation should also take limited preparations for war. To that end, he asked for funds to complete three frigates and to arm merchant vessles. He also asked that the regular army be strengthened and reorganized and that planning for a provisional army begin. Seven months later, in another message to Congress, he suggested that additional taxes be considered to pay for these and other defense measures against the French threat to American commerce. [42]

However, Adams was still not moving toward war quickly enough for the "High Federalists," an important wing of his party which was centered geographically in New England and intellectually around Alexander Hamilton. In early 1798, the retired Secretary of the Treasury wrote personal letters and articles in newspapers signed with pen names pushing for accelerated war preparations. In addition to arming merchant ships and completing the naval vessels already under construction, Hamilton proposed construction of an additional ten ships of the line, fortification of all important ports, suspension by acts of Congress of all treaties with France, licensing of privateers, the creation of a standing army of 20,000 in addition to a provisional army of 30,000 and, of course, new taxes to pay for these heavy expenses. [43] By mid-1798, Fisher Ames, a close ally of Hamilton, was writing to Timothy Pickering, the Federalist Secretary of State, to argue that the Congress lagged far behind the people in its enthusiasm for armaments, and that the public would certainly pay higher taxes for such worthy goals as defense. [44]

The French did nothing to quiet the war fever in the United States. When American envoys reached France, they were met by agents of Talleyrand and presented with a set of mysterious and humiliating demands. They were told that before they could be received officially they would have to apologize for Adams' harsh remarks about France, advance that nation a loan of $12 million, and pay a bribe of $250,000 to Tallyrand and the Directors. The Americans refused, and broke off talks with the unnamed secret agents, designated in their dispatches as X, Y, and Z. In April 1798, when their report to the President and the full diplomatic record was printed in the United States, "the publication of the XYZ dispatches electrified the country as had no other event since the Revolutionary War," in the words of one modern historian. [45]

In this heady atmosphere, Congress passed most of the war program of the High Federalists. A regular and provisional army of 50,000 was created, and George Washington was asked to take command of it. (After some deft maneuvering, Hamilton was able to promote himself to second in command over the claims of more senior former officers of the Continental Army.) The Alien and Sedition Acts were passed, and money was appropriated to complete some warships and begin new ones. All of this was costly. In 1797, the national government had spent about $6 million. By 1798, annual expenses had reached $7.6 million. In 1799, $9.3 million was spent, and $10.8 million in 1800. To meet these extraordinary expenses, new taxes were obviously needed.

In July 1798, only days after passage of the Alien and Sedition Acts and four months after the revelations of the XYZ Affair, Congress passed the direct tax. It was intended to raise $2 million through a tax on land, slaves, and houses. There was little resistance in Congress from the Republicans. Even though they disparaged the seriousness of the threat from France, they could not oppose the tax without seeming to oppose all defense measures. Albert Gallatin was the Republican faction's acknowledged expert on fiscal matters. He had previously favored a permanent direct tax on land and personal property, but was now more concerned to make the temporary character of the new duties explicit. No tax was ever abandoned once it was on the books, he said, and ways would always be found to spend its receipts: "A new regiment, or a few additional frigates, or some new establishments will at any time consume any surplus of revenue which may be at hand." [46] He also suggested that the tax on houses be revised and made progressive, and the rates as enacted did increase from 0.2 percent to 1.0 percent as the value of the house rose.

To collect and enforce the tax, an apparatus was created which would obscure the impact of national control on the subject population. Although federal officials were to assess property and collect the tax, in each state a local board of commissioners was established and given power to make rules for assessment that would reflect local needs and custom. [47] Southern representatives continued to object to the tax on slaves, which clearly had its greatest impact in their region, and many frontier leaders opposed any tax on land. Nonetheless, the bill was passed by the comfortable margin of 62 to 19. [48]

President Adams maintained his caution about the nature and extent of international crisis. He had not asked Congress for the Alien and Sedition Acts, for loans at high interest rates, or for an army of 50,000 men, although he did not veto any of those measures. [49] Nor did he ask Congress for a declaration of war. In fact, in February he named a new representative to France against the advice of his cabinet, all of whom favored

Hamilton's policies of escalation of hostilities with France and continuing rapprochement with Great Britain. Enough Federalist senators objected to the new mission to delay its departure until November, but at that time a three-man delegation left with hopes of reopening direct negotiations.

Even with the President's ambivalence about the scope and imminence of the crisis at hand, opposition throughout the countryside to the direct tax was surprisingly muted, especially when measured against the reaction to the excise four years earlier. But some protest was evident. In January 1799, petitions and complaints were arriving in Congress in large numbers. Although their main point of attack was the Alien and Sedition Acts, which were by far the most unpopular elements in the Federalist war program, petitions usually added a few words in opposition to the new army and the direct tax. In Massachusetts, liberty poles were seen trailing long lists of slogans: "Liberty and Equality — No Stamp Act — No Sedition — No Alien Bills — No Land Tax — Downfall to the Tyrants of America." [50] But the complaints about the new tax were hardly menacing, as one of the High Federalists, Joseph Hale, indicated in a letter to Rufus King: "In the New England States the alien and sedition acts make less noise than the land tax. Its novelty and immediate application to the purse strings excite soft but gentle murmurs." [51]

Protests came also from the South. Jefferson complained that the Federalist program was designed to crush the agrarian economy of his home state, arguing that "of the two millions of Dollars now to be raised by a tax on lands, houses, and slaves, Virginia is to furnish between 3 and 400,000. . . ." [52] Writing in the *City Gazette* of Charleston in 1800, Charles Pinckney resurrected some of the themes from the funding debates: "How then does it happen that in laying a direct tax the whole of it is laid on lands and slaves only, with no other species of property? Why is the whole of it laid on the agricultural interest and the landholder? . . . Why, clearly to exempt all the *monied interest*, which is by far the largest in the Northern states." [53]

At least two noted historians (Hildreth and Morse) and one rather sophisticated political observer (Jefferson) have attributed some part of Federalist electoral losses in 1798 to resentment over the direct tax. Alexander Hamilton seemed to underscore this judgment in a speech to the electors of New York State in 1800 by declaring apologetically that it had never been his party's policy to resort to direct taxation except in the presence of threatened or actual hostilities.[54]

Unlike opposition to the whiskey excise or the Alien and Sedition Acts, all of this protest might well be classified as "soft but gentle murmurs." In one incident, however, resistance to the tax was overt and briefly violent. In Bucks County, Pennsylvania, a group of assessors were evaluating houses when they were captured and detained by a small company of local militia under the leadership of John Fries, a German-American auction cryer. They were admonished not to return to their work, and then released and sent on their way. The historian of the Fries Rebellion (as this incident and its aftermath came to be known) believed that the tax law was unpopular because the federal officers, in addition to assessing houses and land, were also counting windows. Since Congress had repealed the section of the act requiring enumeration of windows, the assessors' activities created the justifiable suspicion that this data was being collected for future taxation.[55]

Some of those involved in harassment of the assessors were captured by federal marshals and put into custody in Bethlehem. A group of 140 men, including horsemen and riflemen, were organized to free the prisoners, but the marshals released them without a struggle, thus avoiding a violent confrontation. In mid-March 1799, less than a week after the incident in Bethlehem, Adams issued the required proclamation, asserting that opposition to the law was carried out by "combinations too powerful to be suppressed in the ordinary course of judicial proceedings," and proceeded to organize a military force to crush this incipient revolution.[56]

When the residents learned of the President's statement and plans, they held a meeting at which they unanimously agreed to cease resistance and permit assessment of their properties. Nonetheless, Adams deployed five hundred men from the regular army, together with nine troops of Pennsylvania militia cavalry. Two thousand militiamen were also asked to stand by in neighboring New Jersey. When the troops arrived, they quickly captured about thirty alleged rebels, including Fries himself, who was conducting an auction. The only casualty of the action was a bull, who was shot while eating out of one of the military wagons; his owner was compensated for damagers incurred. The cost of the whole expedition was estimated at about $80,000, and one officer, writing at the time from Bucks County, said: "this expedition was not only unnecessary, but violently absurd. . . . I do verily believe that a sergeant and six men might have performed all the service for which we have been assembled at so heavy an expense to the United States." [57]

Most of the prisoners, Fries included, were accused of treason and tried in the U.S. circuit court in Philadelphia in May 1799. Some were found guilty, but their convictions were set aside, and they were held for retrial. A year later, Fries and two others were again found guilty, and sentenced to die. Many of the High Federalists were pleased to learn of the convictions, as Timothy Pickering indicated: "Painful as the idea of taking the life of a man, . . . I feel a calm and solid satisfaction that an opportunity is now presented, in executing the just sentence of the law, to crush that spirit, which, if not overthrown and destroyed, may proceed in its career, and overturn the government." [58]

When Adams asked his cabinet how to deal with the convictions, some of its members wanted to execute all three, while others would have been satisfied with killing only Fries. In spite of their opposition to leniency, Adams pardoned everyone convicted of rebellious activities in the brief uprising. During that same month of May, Congress discharged about 3,500 of the armed forces and returned the military to its former status. Expansion of the Navy was also halted, and many of its officers were discharged. The war scare was over. [59]

Though the economic burden of the direct tax was more widespread than the excise, it excited much less controversy. In levying any kind of visible tax for the first time, political leaders might expect resistance from those groups (and there are always some) who felt their share of the burden was over-large. Because of the threat of war with France, opposition to the direct tax of 1798 was muted, and the Jeffersonian Republicans who spoke for such groups in Congress made no serious effort to defeat the tax. But outside of the national capital, perceptions of the menace from France must have been less threatening, and President Adams was unwilling to stir up fears of war among the citizens. So some limited opposition to the tax was evident, in forms ranging from petitions, to liberty poles, to the briefly violent episode in Bucks County. In more normal times, introduction of a new national tax might have provoked much more protest over the national government's expanding extractive system. The threat of war dampened such opposition, but did not altogether eliminate it, since key figures within the elite were themselves uncertain about the seriousness of the danger from the international environment. No such ambiguity existed in 1813, when internal taxes were next imposed.

INTERNAL TAXES AND THE WAR OF 1812

When Albert Gallatin took office as Secretary of the Treasury in 1801, he had four main fiscal goals: a reduction of government expenditures, a balanced budget, a decrease in the size of the national debt, and finally, in response to pressure from Jefferson, alleviation of the tax burden, a goal which obviously conflicted with debt retirement.[60] Although Hamilton had warned that repeal of internal taxes might lead to problems in times of crisis, Gallatin disagreed, arguing that asking people to pay an unwanted tax for no apparent reason during peacetime was hardly the way to condition them to pay more of it cheerfully when an emergency arose. Instead, he felt that it would be better to impose altogether new systems of taxes if and when revenues were needed.[61]

During the first eight years of the Republican era, the Napoleonic Wars in Europe proved to be a great stimulus to American commerce. Even as the great powers on the Continent drove American foreign policy-makers almost mad with harassments, restrictions, and counter-restrictions on U.S. shipping, the merchants were getting rich and so was the Treasury, since import and tonnage duties increased along with trade. The results for Gallatin's policy goals were extraordinary. By 1808, the national debt had been reduced from $80 million to $57 million, even though the unexpected purchase of the Louisiana Territory had added over $11 million to the total. Gallatin had also been able to increase his Treasury reserves from $3 million in 1801 to nearly $14 million by 1808. And all of this had been achieved in the face of repeal of all internal taxes early in Jefferson's first term.[62]

By 1808, harassment of American shipping by British fighting ships was so severe that Gallatin was forced to make preliminary plans for war financing. At that time, he stated unequivocally that no internal taxes would be needed; war costs could be financed by borrowing, since American credit was so firmly established, and tariff revenues would pay for normal expenses of the government. The $14 million reserve Gallatin was holding in his Treasury accounts was no doubt a factor in these sanguine predictions.

That same year, in an attempt to avoid war, Jefferson asked Congress to enact an embargo. By denying permission to export raw materials or finished merchandise to Europe, Jefferson hoped to force the belligerents to recognize American claims of neutral shipping rights. In spite of the stimulus this policy provided for local manufacturing, the commercial classes suffered heavily from the halt in trade under this policy, and their bitter opposition brought about repeal of the embargo shortly before Jefferson left office. During the brief time it had been in effect, its impact on the national government's finances was severe, not only because of increased costs for enforcement of the embargo but because of greatly reduced tax receipts from import and tonnage duties. In 1808, army and navy expenditures were $4.8 million; in 1809, those costs rose to $5.7 million, an increase of about 19 percent. At the same time, revenues from customs duties plummeted from $16.4 million to $7.3 million, a decline of about 55 percent.[63] The lesson was clear, and Gallatin recognized the danger of heavy reliance on revenue from tariff duties: "In time of peace it is almost sufficient to defray the expenses of a war; in time of war, it is hardly competent to support the expenses of a peace establishment." [64]

By 1811, war once again seemed imminent. In November, Madison spoke to Congress. He asserted that British attacks on shipping had "the character as well as the effect of war upon our lawful commerce," and concluded that "Congress will feel the duty of putting the United States into an armor and an attitude demanded by the crisis, and corresponding with the national spirit and expectations." [65] Congress made early preparations for war, including an increase in the size of the army, and Gallatin proposed in a letter to the Chairman of the Ways and Means Committee that excises to yield $2 million be enacted along with a $3 million direct tax.[66]

In June 1812, Madison asked Congress for a declaration of war against Great Britain. After angry debate, the House and Senate approved the resolution, but their votes reflected deep division over the need for war. With such strongly felt reservations, Congress was also hesitant to vote the fiscal measures needed to support the war. The tariff schedule was doubled in 1812, but because of the war's effect on commerce, customs revenues actually dropped by one-half in 1813. Gallatin had earlier received congressional approval to float loans of $11 million, but money was scarce (only $6 million was subscribed) and interest costs were high.[67]

Not until August 1813, when the war was a full year old, did Congress approve a set of internal taxes structured very much like those levied during the Federalist period. A direct tax was designed to collect $3 million, and excise duties were imposed on carriages, sugar refining, and distilled spirits. The taxes as enacted were explicitly labeled in italic letters in the body of the legislation as *"War Taxes,"* and Congress provided for their automatic repeal within a year of the war's end.[68] The direct tax of 1798 as administered by Oliver Wolcott, Hamilton's successor in the Treasury, was designed to take some cognizance of state revenue systems, but little effort was made to do so in the taxes of 1813. However, it was required that each assessor and collector "be a respectable freeholder and reside in the district," and state governments were permitted to assume and pay directly to the Treasury the amounts apportioned to their residents. For relieving the national government of the task of collection in that fashion, a reduction of 15 percent in the total due from each state was granted. In 1814, seven of the states took advantage of this option, and four did so in 1815 and 1816.

In spite of divisions in Congress over the conflict and serious administrative problems involved in creating a brand-new apparatus for tax collection in the midst of a war, yield from the taxes was excellent, and opposition to the new duties was negligible. With no "whiskey boys" to attack collectors or rebellious auctioneers to interrupt revenues, receipts from internal taxes in 1816 were six times as great as those from a similar revenue structure in 1800. More to the point, costs of collecting the taxes (including the 15 percent rebate to some states) were substantially lower than during the Federalist period. Between 1795 and 1801, collection costs for internal taxes ranged from 25 percent (as the collection apparatus was being put together) to a low of 12 percent in 1800. Between 1814 and 1816, costs of collection ranged from only 7.8 percent down to 4.8 percent, an impressive improvement.

The scholar who made these calculations, Henry C. Adams, attributed this happy decline not to any organizational advances in Treasury administration under Gallatin, but to three differences in the environment of collection during the two periods. First, he pointed to what he saw as the disappearance of heavy party and political opposition that was so evident in the Federalist period. Second, he argued that there was more enthusiasm for the war in 1813. Third, he emphasized the temporary nature of the later taxes, and suggested these findings should bring "again clearly to our view how important an element is public sentiment in the working of all revenue systems." [69]

Professor Adams was inaccurate in some important details (both govern-ment officials and the public at large were deeply divided over the War of 1812, as Brown and others show),[70] but his main point was well taken. When taxes were enacted in 1813, there was no question that the nation faced the most severe kind of crisis. While fighting was going on along the nation's periphery in the Great Lakes and on the southern and northern frontiers, the British raided the Atlantic coast, occupied territory in sev-eral states, and burned much of the capital district in their attack on Washington in 1814. In 1798, war was only threatened, and the President was taking steps to try to moderate the dispute between America and France. The duration of the Federalist excise was indefinite, and the expi-ration date of the first direct tax was ambiguous. The war taxes of 1813 were clearly devoted to prosecution of the fighting, and they were just as clearly designed to end as soon as the crisis ended. Indeed, "public sen-timent" was a crucial variable, and that sentiment was influenced first, by the proximity and severity of the crisis, and, second, by the skill with which the political elite was able to relate its actions to that crisis in the public mind. When an unambiguous international crisis was at hand—that is, when no conflict within the elite was apparent over the definition of the situation as critical—citizens who had earlier seen important regime implications in internal taxes of all kinds suspended their opposition and paid those taxes promptly and quietly.

SUMMARY

This brief discussion of internal taxes during the early years of the United States provides some support for a general proposition already put forth: new extractive initiatives are often resisted, sometimes violently, by some portion of the subject population, and governments in turn will often respond with coercion to displays of noncompliance on so vital an issue. At the same time, these events also begin to point out the limits of facile generalization by illustrating that similar initiatives in extractive policy can sometimes result in very different political responses, as times and situa-tions change. In the first ten years after ratification of the Constitution, Alexander Hamilton designed and began to put into effect a full program of internal taxes, including excises and a direct tax. In what seems to be a clear case of regime challenge, the Federalist program was energetically opposed by a broad set of groups, ranging from the Pennsylvania frontiersmen who took part in the Whiskey Rebellion, to the Jeffersonian Republicans in Congress, whose opposition was less violent but equally obdurate. In fact, not until a foreign policy crisis with France made war a real possibility did the Congress approve the direct tax John Adams had requested. When Jefferson became President in 1801, he redeemed his long-time pledge to abolish the internal revenue system, and his party in Congress repealed the excise and direct taxes.

In 1813, Madison and Gallatin requested approval of an almost identical system of internal taxes. But instead of provoking the kind of widespread opposition and conflict that had surrounded the Federalist program and its implementation, Congress quietly passed the tax legislation, and internal duties were efficiently collected throughout the country. The explanation for this abrupt change in patterns of political behavior is hardly mysterious. The nation was in the midst of a full-scale war with England, and its survival was at stake. In the face of that unambiguous crisis, an issue which had previously been seen to imply a serious expansion in the national regime's extractive capacity met with no significant opposition for the duration of the war.

4 / THE TARIFF

IN STRIKING CONTRAST to the dispute over internal taxes, early tariff policy aroused no heated debate within the political elite, and no difficulties arose with collections. The issue of a national tariff had been widely discussed since 1781, and most Americans agreed that lack of such revenue authority was a crucial defect in the Articles of Confederation. The new Constitution specifically denied import duties to the states and reserved that revenue source for the central government, so by imposing such taxes the Congress did not increase the total tax burden on the subject population. Merchants simply sent their import duties to a different Treasury.

As a source of revenues for the national government, the tariff was widely accepted. But as a new policy goal—protection of manufactures—crept into the extractive system, the South began to complain that the regime was undergoing unwarranted transformation, and that new burdens were now borne by their region. Concern over the reallocation of burdens and benefits provoked concern in the South about the protection of slavery and their own distinctive social system, and South Carolina created the doctrine of nullification to preserve Southern veto power over changes in the scope and character of the regime. With a combination of concessions on the tariff and threats of force, Andrew Jackson and other political leaders mollified the South and discredited nullification as a constitutional remedy.

NORMAL POLITICS AND THE TARIFF, 1789–1816

When measured against such grand fights as those involving the impost of 1781, funding and assumption, or the excise, "the tariff . . . aroused very little opposition" when it was passed in 1789, according to one student of public opinion during the Federalist era.[1] Since the need for steady revenues was obvious, the First Congress turned very quickly to consideration of tax measures. Madison proposed that the nation adopt the basic plan developed (but never adopted) under the Confederation: a 5 percent ad valorem duty (based on valuation of a commodity) for most products, along with specific duties (based on the quantity of a good imported, and levied by the pound, ton, barrel, etc.) on a smaller number of products, such as tea, coffee, and sugar. Madison argued that there was no feasible alternative to raising revenues through tariff duties:

> There are but two objects to which, in this dilemma we can have recourse—direct taxation and excises. Direct taxation is not contemplated by any gentleman on this floor, nor are our constituents prepared for such a system of revenue; they expect that it will not be applied to until it is found that sufficient funds cannot be obtained in any other way. Excise would give particular disgust in some States, therefore gentlemen will not make up the deficiency from that quarter.[2]

Some states, such as Massachusetts and Pennsylvania, had previously enacted higher rates in their own tariff schedules to protect local industries, and wanted increased duties on those favored items continued in the national tariff. For example, Congressman Bland of Virginia proposed a duty of 3¢ a bushel on imported coal to help the mines in his district. Most such amendments were accepted by the rest of Congress, and what may have been the first logrolling coalition under the new Constitution passed higher specific duties (up to 50 percent of the cost of some goods) on hemp, cordage, nails, indigo, tobacco, and manufactures of iron and glass. Ad valorem duties were also increased on some manufactured items, such as iron castings, gunpowder, and ready-made clothing.

Luxuries were also burdened with higher taxes. Carriages paid the highest rate of 15 percent; china, gold and silver leaf, and shoe buckles carried a 10 percent duty; and saddles, fur hats, brushes, and walking sticks paid 7.5 percent. Items on the free list—which paid no duties— included saltpeter (for the local manufacture of gunpower), tin, lead, wool, cotton, raw hides and skins, and dyestuffs. Madison argued hard for a duty on molasses, pointing out that, "it will be best to lay our hands upon the duty by charging this article upon its importation, to avoid a more disagreeable measure"—an excise on distilled spirits. Indeed, one tariff historian believes that members of the First Congress were so opposed to internal taxes that they "were ready to agree to almost any import duty rather than resort to the other mode of taxation." [3] The House decided on a high duty of 6¢ a gallon for molasses, but the Senate reduced that rate to 2.5¢ a gallon.

There was controversy around the Revenue Act of 1789, but it did not concern the enactment of tariff duties. Tonnage duties, which were levied on importing ships according to their gross size and were paid in addition to tariff taxes, were also at issue. At the outset, Madison argued for what one historian has called:

> . . . the enactment of an American navigation system—designed to supersede the navigation systems erected by the individual states during the period of the Articles of Confederation—by which American ships would be favored in American ports over foreign vessels, the goods imported into the United States in American ships would pay less duty than similar goods carried by foreign ships, and the coastwise trade would be reserved to ships flying the American flag. [4]

These proposals, similar to the system Great Britain had maintained during the colonial period, were not controversial, and were enacted promptly.

But Madison also suggested incorporating into this structure a provision discriminating in favor of countries which had concluded commercial treaties with the United States. That proposal was frankly designed to help France and penalize Great Britain. French ships would have been required to pay only 30¢ per ton upon entry into an American port, while English vessels would have paid twice as much. Hamilton, still a lawyer and private citizen living in New York City, was opposed to Madison's plan. His admiration for Great Britain and distaste for France was well known, but his public arguments did not restate those preferences, but pointed instead to potential revenue problems. Economic warfare of this type, he argued, could lead to severe reductions in British trade, which made up the bulk of American imports. The unintended result would be a fall in tariff collections. Merchants engaged in trade with England also protested to Congress, but the House of Representatives still passed Madison's plan. However, the Senate soon removed the discrimination against British commerce, and the tonnage act, as passed in 1789, made no distinction between ships of foreign nations, all of which were dealt with less favorably than ships which were either owned or built by Americans.

The public reaction to the new taxes was mild. As one historian describes it:

> The test of popular sentiment was gloriously successful. Instead of exciting opposition, the revenue act dispelled it. Men of anti-Federal opinions as well as the friends of the Constitution united in praising it and its beneficial effects. . . . References to the workings of the law are rare in the publications of the period, but the absence of criticism is of itself a sufficient proof that the measure was not unpopular.[5]

There are at least three good reasons for that quiescence in the face of the concrete economic impact of that legislation. First, under the Articles of Confederation, all states had levied import duties and tonnage charges. Except for Massachusetts, which repealed its navigation laws in 1786, the states retained those taxes until they were preempted by the national government in 1789. So citizens did not suddenly find themselves paying taxes where there had been none before. Second, tariff duties were relatively invisible because they did not appear as a separate charge, like a modern sales tax, but were absorbed into and raised the total price of imported goods. Third, and most important, the public *expected* to pay federal tariff duties under the new regime. A national tariff had been frequently discussed—and almost enacted—during the Confederation period; the constitutional provision forbidding the states the use of that tax emphasized that the national government was planning to make full use of that source of revenues; and proponents of the new Constitution, from the authors of the *Federalist* on down, made it abundantly clear that the major source of funds for the general government would be import taxes. For all those reasons, both the elite and the mass public assumed the continued existence of tariffs in some moderate but otherwise poorly defined range of rates.

Some rough idea of the settled character of these expectations can be gauged from the high rate of compliance with those tax levies. Merchants in Philadelphia voluntarily entered into a compact to prevent smuggling, which had been rampant in the recent history of the colonies and states. Throughout the country, there was "substantial compliance within shipping and merchantile circles," [6] perhaps a sign of the gratitude of the commercial class, which was getting important benefits from the new government, including protection against competition from foreign shipping, interest payments from the national debt, and the services of the national bank. Whatever the reason, their present behavior was in striking contrast to their past activities, and their cooperation helped make customs collections relatively efficient. During the first twenty-five years of the nation's life, the average cost of collecting customs duties was a bit under 4 percent of gross receipts, only a little higher than the 3 percent reported three-quarters of a century later in 1884.[7]

Other evidence is available to demonstrate the uncontroversial nature of the tariff and its collection. Appointments to office in the customs service were handled routinely. Of the 136 posts to be filled in the federal customs service, 61 seemed to have had close equivalents in state customs services. Of those, the state incumbent was given that federal post in 69 percent of the cases, in 7 percent of the cases they were given some other post in the national service, and in only one quarter of the cases were they given no federal job.[8] Party affiliation was not an important criterion for officeholding, and turnover in personnel in the customs service was almost entirely the result of death or resignation, rather than partisan removal. By the time Gallatin took office in 1801, the customs staff was highly professional, and functioned capably under the direction of the Treasury Secretary's immediate subordinates.[9]

The customs service was also an impressive model of administrative efficiency. Hamilton was careful to limit as closely as possible his collectors' discretion in the valuation of goods and property, and he maintained tight control of his large organization. Leonard White describes the agency's operations thus:

> The customs service under Hamilton was the best example of the administrative ideal of the Federalist party. The new government started with an old tradition of tax evasion. . . . Hamilton directed the collectors to start suit on delinquent importers' bonds the very day they became overdue. He exacted a weekly report of collections

and regular settlements with the Treasury. Without hesitation he removed an occasional delinquent or dilatory collector. He sharply reprimanded one who had initiated an unauthorized expenditure for a local customs building. He denied the collectors any right to make their own interpretations of the revenue laws, and required all of them to observe the interpretations which came in a steady stream from his pen. At the same time he enjoined strict fairness and impartiality towards all importers and shipowners, encouraged the collectors by commendation, and sought to improve their scales of pay.[10]

White contrasts this performance with the Foreign Service in the young nation, which was an administrative nightmare, and with the British civil service, where at that time offices were sold outright, the civil list was a repository for the aristocracy's friends and bastards, and revenue collections were slow and uncertain. When measured against these models, Hamilton's customs service looks very much like an early prototype of a modern bureaucracy, carrying out its routine tasks with striking efficiency. Under the presidencies of Jefferson and Madison, both the organization of the individual customshouses and the administrative procedures of the service as a whole remained essentially unchanged.[11]

The tariff schedule was revised by Congress twelve times between 1789 and the War of 1812. To meet the government's increasing revenue needs, rates were increased by one-half on specified duties in 1790. The tariff act of May 1792 enacted eighteen of the twenty-one proposals for revisions that Hamilton had made in the *Report on Manufactures* (including a direct subsidy to fisheries) and thereby raised the overall rate of specified duties to about 13.5 percent. Describing the tariff situation in 1794, an historian makes it clear that an era of normalcy was at hand:

> We have now reached a period where the financial policy of the government was fully established and when discussion of abstract principles of taxation ceased for a long time. Numerous changes in the revenue law were required and were made. Twenty-four acts modifying the duty on foreign imports more or less were passed during the twenty-two years between the act of 1794 and the general revision of the tariff of 1816. With two or three exceptions, they had no other motive than to adjust the revenue to the needs of the Treasury.[12]

Important increases were made in 1797, 1800, and 1804, all of them justified by increased demand for revenue to meet new problems—frontier defense, foreign complications, or the needs of the funding system. Trade expanded rapidly because of the war in Europe, and receipts from customs duties were so high that by 1806 Jefferson and Gallatin were pondering a new problem—what to do with revenues above and beyond those committed to retirement of the debt. (In a little over a year, the Emargo Act of 1807 ended this unaccustomed prosperity in the Treasury.)

A minor exception to the tariff pattern was the salt duty, imposed at the end of a special session of Congress in 1797 as part of early preparations for possible war with France. This tax was considered highly discriminatory by the agrarian sector, since it represented such a large part of the cost of salt and since large quantities of that product were required for livestock feed. Although Jefferson advocated the repeal of the duty as early as 1802, he did so with little urgency, and Gallatin, who opposed the tax on political and ideological grounds, was nonetheless anxious to retain the $500,000 it contributed annually to the Treasury. In March 1807, the salt tax was finally repealed, the only important duty removed from the tariff schedule during this period.

In sum, throughout these twenty-five years, the national tariff, which had been the object of such serious dispute under the Articles of Confederation, was not a public issue at all, even though its rates climbed steadily and incrementally until they were in many instances several times their initial level. Although the first tariff was moderate in its rates and mildly protective in its impact, protection was not the argument for increases, as it was in later, more bitter tariff battles. Instead, the government asked for higher duties to meet growing revenue needs over the years. Within the parameters of established extractive policy, the political elite quietly and ably adjusted revenue schedules to meet fiscal requirements in an era when tariff politics raised no new questions about the limits of the American regime.

THE PROTECTIVE TARIFF: 1816–1833

After the War of 1812, the quiet course of tariff politics ended. Although import duties still supplied almost all of the nation's revenues, the tariff was also used in explicit support of a new policy goal—protection for American manufactured goods and for some agricultural products; and the struggle over the tariff's uses and consequences brought the nation to the brink of an authority crisis in the years between 1828 and 1833. The

South, forced by its defeats on the tariff to take stock of its position in the Union, began to realize that the survival of its economic base—the slave system—was threatened as well. Thus the Civil War grew closer.

But in 1816, those dangers were a long way off. The United States had just settled a painful war with Great Britain, a war which had provided a strong impetus for nationalism in America. Specific nationalist proposals, such as those for a new Bank of the United States and for better roads and waterways, were offered to remedy the nation's weaknesses as they had been exposed in wartime. The War of 1812 had also accelerated the development of manufacturing, as the Embargo Act had done a few years earlier. New industry had grown up all over the country: cotton mills made cloth in New England; foundries smelted steel in Pittsburgh; farmers grew hemp in Kentucky, where it was woven into bagging; and wool was an important item of commerce in Vermont and Ohio.[13] European manufacturers had lost control of the growing American market, but they were sufficiently anxious to regain that influence to contemplate sacrifices for such purposes. Thus, in Great Britain, Lord Brougham explained to Parliament in 1816 that recent heavy exports to America were useful, and that it was "well worth while to incure a loss upon the first exportation, in order, by the glut, to stifle in the cradle those rising manufactures in the United States, which war had forced into existence, contrary to the natural course of things." [14]

Many leaders, therefore, felt that those young industries needed protection, although there was far less consensus about how much protection was necessary, and for what items. Indeed, with the war over, the revenue system needed reform since most of the internal taxes enacted to support military costs were no longer necesary. As part of that overall reform, and in conjunction with the postwar tax reduction, President Madison suggested in December 1815 that congress consider protective tariffs:

> Under circumstances giving a powerful impulse to manufacturing industry it has made among us a progress and exhibited an efficiency which justify the belief that with a protection not more than is due to the enterprising citizens whose interests are now at stake it will become at an early day not only safe against occasional competitions from abroad, but a source of domestic wealth and even of external commerce. . . .[15]

Alexander Dallas, the Secretary of the Treasury, submitted a set of proposals which, reverberating with echoes of Hamilton's famous *Report on*

Manufactures, recommended protective duties on commodities such as cotton and woolen products at levels substantially higher than prewar tariffs, but lower than the wartime schedule of taxes.

The chairman of the House Ways and Means Committee, William Lowndes of South Carolina, reported out a bill that closely followed the Dallas proposals. It recommended a reduction in tariffs from their peaks during the war, but the new schedule would be 42 percent higher than those duties in existence prior to the war. In addition to the increased taxes on cotton products and woolens, it also incorporated a proposal to establish a "minimum" by valuing at 25¢ a square yard any cotton cloth whose original cost was less than that figure. This ingenious device for protecting American cloth from competition from India was originally suggested by Francis C. Lowell, proprietor of one of the largest and most efficient mills in Boston.[16] But Lowell's protectionism was moderate and selective, and he had imparted that philosophy to his young friend, Daniel Webster, who was then a congressman representing Portsmouth, New Hampshire. Lowell's efficient mills could survive with lower duties on cotton cloth than those proposed in the bill. Moreover, Webster's New Hampshire constituents included a number of shippers and merchants engaged in the India trade, so it was natural for him to oppose heavy protective tariffs. But his attempt to decrease duties by steps in future years failed, and the best he could do for his mercantile constituency was an amendment exempting from the new tariffs the cargoes of any ship already underway for America.[17]

The only other clash of any magnitude over the bill occurred when John Randolph of Roanoke led a brief foray against the "minimum." Randolph was an agrarian free trader, and opposed any federal support for manufacturers who, he believed, acquired their wealth at the expense of the agricultural sector. Randolph's efforts provoked John C. Calhoun, then congressman from South Carolina, to speak on behalf of the tariff, and his youthful statements in support of protection reappeared in later years to embarrass him in his subsequent struggle against the tariff. In 1816, he supported the protective tariff primarily as a means of war reconstruction and as a gesture of support for and unity with the other sections of the nation, and he argued that it would provide a new and more powerful cement to make the parts of the nation adhere more closely. He also added a brief reproach to Randolph and those others who hoped to keep the nation agricultural: "Neither agriculture, manufactures, nor com-

merce, separately is the cause of wealth; it flows from the three combined. Without commerce, industry would have no stimulus; without
manufactures, it would be without the means of production; and without
agriculture, neither of the others can subsist." [18]

The attempt to strike out the "minimum" failed by a vote of 82 to 51.
Not long afterwards, the bill itself passed by the substantial margin of 88
to 54. Party lines did not seem particularly salient; the Republicans cast
63 votes for the bill and 31 against it, while the Federalists voted 25 in
favor and 23 against it. Moreover, sectional divisions were only faintly visible in the House balloting. The eight states of the South then represented in Congress split widely, casting 25 votes for the bill and 39
against, with strong support for the tariff in Kentucky, and a majority in
favor in South Carolina and Tennessee. New England was also badly split,
with 17 votes for the bill and 10 against. Strong sectional solidarity was
discernible only in the middle states of New York, Pennsylvania, New Jersey, and Delaware, which cast 42 ballots for the bill and only 5 against,
and in Ohio, which cast all of its 4 votes in favor of the tariff. [19] The bill
quickly passed the Senate, where protectionist sentiment was stronger,
and the President signed it only thirty-nine days after it was introduced in
the House of Representatives.

If the tariff of 1816 was not the obvious product of either sectional or
party cleavages, neither was it passed by a classical logrolling coalition.
Some members, like Randolph, voted steadily against protection and for
reductions in duties; others voted consistently for protective tariffs; but
the votes of many members shifted, and some among them seemed to
embody what one tariff historian called the "jealousy of the partisans of
particular industries and their intolerance towards the interests of distant
states." As illustration, he pointed to the objections of Northern members
to a high duty on sugar, which was countered by Southern complaints
about protection for cotton manufactures. And on the question of protection for iron, both the North and the South united against the Middle
States. [20]

As the pattern of logrolling on tariffs which had been evident between
1789 and 1816 began to crumble, John Calhoun predicted with startling
foresight that those jealousies would probably increase because a tariff that
went beyond revenue needs to protection would soon be regarded as "an
immense tax on one portion of the community to put money into the
pockets of another." [21] The beneficiaries would obviously be the manufac-

turers; it was less clear who would bear the main burden of the taxes, but Randolph thought he knew: "On whom bears the duty on coarse woolens and linens and blankets, upon salt and all the necessaries of life? On poor men and on slaveholders." [22] In years to come, little would be heard from the poor, but the slaveholders would come forward with impassioned indictments of the tariff's unfair impact and bitter resistance to increased protection.

In fact, the 1816 tariff was only mildly protective. F. W. Taussig, a leading tariff historian, even argued that, "the act of 1816, which is generally said to mark the beginning of a distinctly protective policy in this country, belongs rather to the earlier series of acts, beginning with that of 1789," and suggested that "no strong popular movement for protection can be traced before the crisis of 1818–19." [23] The lack of a well-disciplined, logrolling majority is one reason why the act was less protective than some manufacturers had hoped. But it was also true that the shipping and mercantile community, which generally opposed increased tariffs which might reduce trade, was at that time of equal or greater political consequence than the manufacturing sector, as Daniel Webster's policy stance indicated. Later, as the balance between those interests shifted, and as manufacturing spread through the West and New England, the protective thread which had been apparent even in the tariff of 1789 became dominant, tariffs increased, and those who believed themselves the victims of this policy began to draw together and offer stiffer resistance to it.

The next skirmish over the tariff took place in 1820 when, impelled by the panic of 1819 and the depression that followed, businessmen and manufacturers renewed their appeals for protection. The House Committee on Manufactures suggested a general increase in the entire tariff schedule of about 5 percent, and proposed even higher duties for cotton and woolen cloth, ready-made clothing, iron, and hemp. In addition, higher duties on sugar, molasses, coffee, and salt were requested to meet increased revenue needs. The bill passed the House in April by a vote of 91 to 78, and by combining that vote and an earlier roll call it is possible to gauge the opinion of all but nine of the Representatives. Once again, the middle states of New York, Pennsylvania, New Jersey, and Delaware provided the bulk of the tariff's support, with 55 of those members voting yes and only 1 opposing the legislation. New England was still uncertain, and divided almost evenly, with 19 in favor of protection and 18 opposed.

The western states of Ohio, Illinois, and Indiana were unanimous in favor of the revisions, but their 8 votes were not yet an important bloc. But in the South, solidarity in opposition was growing; members from that section of the country cast only 8 votes in favor of higher tariffs, while 63 of their number opposed them. Before the Revolution, the British navigation system had been overhauled to provide revenues as well as protection for commerce, and opposition arose in the colonies. In much the same way, the changing policy goals of the tariff, which now extended beyond revenues to protection, were beginning to transform patterns of support for those taxes.

Although the South was growing closer to unanimity in its opposition to the tariff, the arguments its spokesmen put forth were hardly original, and were primarily based on the old Jeffersonian dogma about the necessity for maintaining the social primacy of agriculture in the United States. Typical was Representative William Archer of Virginia, who opposed the protective tariff because he opposed manufacturing:

> . . . the objection of the greatest force to an extended manufacturing system related to the character of the population it had a tendancy to form. What kind of population was it? A population distorted and decrepit as respects both bodily and mental endowments, equally marked by imbecility and abasement. How unlike our ancestors achieving the Revolution! . . . Among civilized nations the heated and surcharged atmosphere of extensive manufacturing establishments was found to present the situation most unfavorable to moral sanity. [24]

Later in the year in a speech in Boston, Daniel Webster repeated the same theme in his continuing opposition to protection. Agriculture, he believed, was more conducive to the growth of social well-being and "individual respectability and happiness" than employment in manufacturing, and he praised the life and moral standards of the rural freeholder: "He thereby obtains a feeling of respectability, a sense of propriety and of personal independence which is generally essential to elevated character. He has a stake in society and is inclined therefore, rather to uphold it than to demolish it."

Webster believed that the opposite was true of factory workers in Europe: "They have no stake in society; they hang loose upon it, and are often neither happy in their condition nor without danger to the state." [25]

A more novel argument against protection began to surface, if only in a tentative form, during the debate in 1820. The proposition, made almost offhandedly by Representative Ezekiel Whitman of Massachusetts, was that protection lay outside the established goals of the regime because taxation was constitutionally authorized only for revenue purposes:

> What originated the government of the United States? Was it specifically constituted with a view to manufactures? Is there any specific delegation of power in our constitution for this object? Have we even any direct control over manufacturing establishments? . . . Hitherto we conducted the affairs of this nation with some view to the original design of this government. We have been content generally to do that which we were distinctly and explicitly authorized to do, namely, to regulate commerce—external commerce and commerce between the States.[26]

Henry Clay, a strong proponent of protection, answered Whitman and pointed out that the constitutional argument found no support elsewhere in the House:

> The honorable gentleman professes to be a friend to manufactures! And yet he has found an insurmountable constitutional impediment to their encouragement, of which, as no other gentleman has relied upon it, I shall leave him in the undisturbed possession.[27]

Other opponents of protection began to take up the constitutional argument. For example, Webster used it in the speech quoted above, saying that he doubted that protection was constitutional unless it resulted "*incidentally* only" from duties levied "for the leading purpose of revenue." [28] Northern complaints about the protective tariff were based primarily on fears that one functional interest—manufacturing—would be favored over agriculture or commerce and shipping by the activities of the national government; and, as later shifts of opinion in the North indicate, those fears were not nearly as deep-seated as those developing in the South, where farsighted politicians were beginning to realize that their whole social system might someday come under attack. But in either case, a small segment of the political elite was beginning to treat the protective tariff as a regime issue. Initial agreement over the scope of the state's extractive system was based on its need for adequate revenues, not on the requirements of Northern manufacturers for protection. Thus, the tariff's new policy goals were disrupting settled coalitions and planting the seed of conflict which reached its fullest flower years later in South Carolina's attempt to nullify the tariff.

As Charles Sydnor points out, the Southern states had social bases for their growing sectional consciousness:

> . . . all ten of the states below Mason and Dixon's line and the Ohio River had certain things in common. All were predominantly agricultural, and in many areas the producing unit was the plantation—a social, governmental, and economic world in itself. There was a widespread interest in the export of staples to distant markets. There was the problem of two dissimilar races living in the same land. Slavery as a system of labor and of social control was of concern to every state. And there were traditions and attitudes and institutions that were the result of these regional traits. Of course, none of these characteristics had the same force in every small part of the South, but there were no Southern states that did not feel their force. [29]

Political events were also contributing to the growth of Southern consciousness. In 1820, during the fierce debate over the extension of slavery that surrounded the admission of Missouri as a state, prescient politicians saw a future which promised nothing but insecurity for the South. John Quincy Adams felt that the debate over the Tallmadge amendment had disclosed a grim secret: ". . . it revealed the basis for a new organization of parties. . . . Here was a new party ready formed, . . . terrible to the whole Union, but portentuously terrible to the South—threatening in its progress the emancipation of all their slaves, threatening in its immediate effect that Southern domination which has swayed the Union for the last twenty years. . . ." [30]

The census of 1820 and the reapportionment that followed it reinforced the South's fears, even while it added strength to those forces favoring protection. In the decade from 1810 to 1820, the ten states of the South grew at a rate of 28 percent while the rest of the country increased its population by 38 percent. While the South in 1810 had constituted 47 percent of the nation's population, by 1820 its share had dropped to 45 percent. And the decline in relative importance was even more marked in the five states on the Atlantic coast—Maryland, North Carolina, South Carolina, Virginia, and Georgia—that were the South when the Union was formed. Their growth in that decade was only 15 percent, and their share of the nation's population dropped from 36 to 31 percent. [31]

The South was slowly becoming a minority, and its most perceptive political leaders saw the dangers entailed by that status. If the national government could put aside the constraints of the strict-constructionists' interpretation of the Constitution, a majority in Congress could do almost anything. John Randolph made the point bitterly during the 1824 debate on the general survey bill, which was meant as a first step toward a broad program of internal improvements:

> If Congress possesses the power to do what is proposed by this bill, they may emancipate every slave in the United States. . . . And where will they find the power? They may . . . hook the power upon the first loop they find in the Constitution; they might take the preamble—perhaps the war making power—or they might take a greater sweep, and say, with some gentlemen, that it is not to be found in this or that of the granted powers, but results from all of them—which is not only a dangerous but *the most* dangerous doctrine.[32]

Moreover, the reapportionment of 1820 had affected the balance of strength on the tariff issue. Those areas which had been overwhelming in favor of the tariff of 1816—New York, Pennsylvania, and the western states—gained 28 seats in the House, while the South, where opposition was most vigorous, gained much less. Eight of the twelve senatorial seats added since 1816 went to regions where protection was popular.[33] At the same time, protectionists were making themselves heard at the White House. In the annual messages delivered in 1822 and in 1823 (the latter included what came to be known as the Monroe Doctrine), the President had given cautious support to higher protective tariffs. Finally, Henry Clay, whose "American system" included protection as one of its key elements, was empowered as Speaker to select the chairmen of congressional committees. It was, therefore, no surprise that John Tod of Pennsylvania, head of the Committee on Manufactures in 1824, was an ardent protectionist, and that he reported out a bill increasing duties on cotton goods (including bagging), woolens and wool, iron, hemp, flax, and molasses in January of that year.

Since the Treasury had shown a surplus for the two previous years, no pretense was made that the increases were required to raise revenues and, in Monroe's messages, revenue needs and protection were discussed separately and without interconnection. In fact, the debate made it clear that most congressmen had no idea what the effect of the proposed bill might be on revenues. Representative Churchill C. Cambreleng of New York, who was considered "a great authority on financial subjects," predicted that the revenue system would be "seriously injured" by the measure, and P. P. Barbour of Virginia agreed that its effect would be to reduce revenues. On the other hand, Tod, chairman of the committee offering the bill, suggested that revenues would increase under it for three years or a bit longer, but hedged by stating that even if this estimate were incorrect the legislation was badly needed. Henry Clay was straightforward on the question; he said that estimates of the bill's effects on revenues were nothing but conjecture, but that he thought the bill was so necessary that if new revenues were needed to offset its effects, he would support an excise—and this in a presidential election year! [34]

With protection the only possible justification for the tariff increase, the bill's opponents once again invoked regime arguments against it. The issue was first raised by Barbour of Virginia, who conceded that the letter of the Constitution was not violated, but asked "whether we do not in effect transcend the limits of our legitimate authority as much by the exercise of a granted power for a purpose for which it was not granted as by the exercise of a power not granted. I answer that we do." In response, Clay pointed out that the only limitation on the power to lay duties and imposts was that they be uniform throughout the United States, and went on to state: "The gentleman from Virginia has, however, entirely mistaken the clause of the Constitution on which we rely. It is that which gives to Congress the power to regulate commerce with foreign nations. The grant is plenary, without any limitations whatever and includes the whole power of regulation of which the subject to be regulated is susceptible. It is as full and complete a grant of power as is that to declare war." [35]

With the regime issue now fully exposed, the debate continued. Strong opposition came from the South, with Representatives James Hamilton Jr., Joel Poinsett, and George McDuffie from South Carolina taking prominent roles. But the most eloquent argument against the tariff came from Daniel Webster, who no longer represented New Hampshire with its shipping interests, but was now congressman from Boston. Although Massachusetts was beginning to turn to manufactures, the financiers, shippers, and merchants of Boston were not yet ready to embrace protection wholeheartedly, and they told Webster so when he circularized fifty of his most prominent constituents. They objected most strenuously to the proposed increases on iron, hemp, and flax, which were products of importance to shipowners, and to the duty on molasses, which would hurt New England's rum industry and its trade with the West Indies. With that guidance, Webster made an inspired plea for free trade, using rhetoric and logic so compelling that he had trouble refuting it in later years when he turned to support of protection.[36]

All the eloquence was to no avail. The bill passed the House on April 16 by a vote of 107 to 102, and the Senate by a margin of 25 to 21 a month later. Once again the South was solidly against it, with support coming only from Kentucky and Tennessee, states which were still as much Western as Southern in their outlook. The rest of the West was unanimously in favor of the increases. Strong support came from the middle states while New England was divided evenly in the Senate, and voted about three to one in favor of the bill in the House.

In spite of some conservative amendments in the Senate, the bill as passed was "a distinctively protective piece of legislation." [37] Increased duties were voted for iron, lead, wool, hemp, cotton bagging, and textile fabrics, with the new duties averaging almost 37 percent. Only the woolen manufacturers were unhappy; the duty on woolen imports had been increased from 25 to 33⅓ percent, but this increased protection was offset by a substantial increase in the duty on raw wool, which had previously been taxed at only 15 percent and now had to bear duties of 30 percent. Although the tariff of 1824 could harldy be considered a complete triumph for every segment of the protectionist movement, its passage was "the decisive battle of a campaign that had long been waging," according to one tariff historian.[38]

With the success of that campaign came even broader support. Ignoring the strong opposition to protection evidenced by the Massachusetts delegation in the votes on the bill, President John Quincy Adams seemed to move toward acceptance of the protective principle. Moreover, his appointments indicated that protectionists had captured the executive branch. With Henry Clay as Secretary of State, a high-tariff advocate sat at Adams' right hand in the cabinet; and Richard Rush, the new Secretary of the Treasury, submitted a letter to Congress in 1825 which was enthusiastically protectionist:

> By a flourishing state of manufactures, we shall see rising up a new class of capitalists, rivaling in the extent and usefulness of their operations, and in the amount of their gains, the wealthiest of our merchants. . . . When to the complete establishment of manufactures,

the internal improvements of the country shall have been super-
added, the farmer of the United States cannot but perceive that the
measure of his prosperity is made potentially full.[39]

Daniel Webster, the most convincing opponent of protection, was also
"the most trustworthy barometer for the climate of opinion in State
Street," Boston's business center. In 1825, the great firm of W. and S.
Lawrence of Boston turned its interest and capital from importing to
domestic manufacturing, and the rest of State Street fell in behind it. So
did Daniel Webster, who was now to become the Congress' most eloquent supporter of protection.[40] As one modern historian has put it,
Webster "was poised to represent, as precisely as he could, the balance of
contending interests at home. When that balance should swing to the protectionist side, so would he."[41]

While the supporters of protection were increasing their strength, the
opponents of the tariff were becoming more militant, especially in the
state of South Carolina. As early as 1824, members of the South Carolina
state legislature considered a set of motions restating the principles of
strict construction and arguing that the protective tariff and internal improvements were unconstitutional. Because Calhoun's conversion from
these nationalist policies was not yet complete, his supporters opposed
the measures, which were passed by the state senate and tabled by the assembly. Only a year after passage of the new tariff, massive speculation
forced the price of cotton down from 32¢ in June 1825 to 13¢ in October.
With that painful blow to South Carolina's economy, and with the energetic guidance of William Smith, an arch-opponent of the Calhoun faction
in South Carolina, the state legislature passed the resolutions. Calhoun
seemed to be almost alone in his own state.[42]

The protectionists pushed ahead. Badly hurt by competition from Great
Britain, New England mill owners met in Boston in September 1826, and
called for help in the form of increased tariffs on woolen goods. In January
1827, Congressman Rollin Mallary of Vermont, the chairman of the
House Committee on Manufactures, introduced a woolens bill which did
not change the ad valorem rate of duty on woolen goods—it remained at
33⅓ percent—but established three "minima" for those products. With
Webster's vigorous support, the bill passed the House on February 10 by
a margin of 106 to 95, but it was quickly destroyed in the Senate, where
the South was stronger. Its final defeat came on a tie vote where Calhoun,

maneuvered by Van Buren into declaring himself, cast the deciding vote against the bill. Calhoun was following the lead of his state, which was now in the forefront of opposition to the principle of protection, and he was reflecting the special pain that Southern planters felt at increased duties on coarse woolens, an import primarily used for clothing of slaves.[43]

To solidify the organization of their interests and broaden their base of support, the protectionists called together a convention in July 1827 under the aegis of the Pennsylvania Society for the Promotion of Manufactures. Attending that meeting in Harrisburg were growers, editors and publicists (Hezekiah Niles and Matthew Carey), manufacturers (Abbot Lawrence of Massachusetts), and a clutch of politicians (among them two United States Senators and a number of congressmen, including Chairman Mallary of the Committee on Manufactures). After five days of discussions, the conferees recommended increased duties and new minima on woolens.

At the same time the protectionists were planning their legislative strategy, opponents of the tariff in South Carolina were escalating the level of their rhetorical attacks. For his series of essays, Robert J. Turnbull, a tidewater planter, took his title from Tom Paine's famous pamphlets in support of the American Revolution. Turnbull's articles, called *The Crisis*, set out the Southern view that loose construction, the tariff, and the future of slavery were all interconnected. Concerned by the broadened interpretations of the "general welfare" clause in the Constitution, Turnbull pointed out how that construction could be used to undermine the slave base of the Southern economy:

> . . . these words "general welfare" are becoming every day more and more important to the folks, who are now so peaceably raising their cotton and rice, between the *Little Pedee* and the *Savannah*.[*] The question, it must be recollected, is not simply whether we are to have a foreign commerce. It is not simply whether we are to have splendid national works, in which we have no interest, executed chiefly at our cost. . . . It is not whether we are to be taxed without end. . . . But the still more interesting question is, whether the institutions of our forefathers . . . are to be preserved . . . free from the rude hands of innovators and enthusiasts, and from the molestation or interference of any legislative power on earth but our own?

* The two rivers that bounded South Carolina on the north and the south.

Or whether, like the weak, the dependent, and the unfortunate colonists of the West-Indies, we are to drag on a miserable state of political existence, constantly vibrating between our hopes and our fears, as to what a Congress may do towards us, without any accurate knowledge of our probable fate, and without a hope of successful resistance.[44]

Turnbull's conclusion was that South Carolina should resist—forcibly, if necessary—those federal laws which its citizens believed were in violation of the limits of the Constitution. And he called for courage in that struggle:

Never, never since the colonization of the country has any measure been adopted, no, not the odious stamp act of England, which demands from the Southern States, a more steady and a more determined resistance than this tariff; not a resistance by resolutions of town meetings, but by such acts and measures of the local Legislatures, as shall curse the usurpers at Washington, to tremble at what they are doing, and to pause, ere they plunge this people, hitherto so happy and so united, into discord and disunion. Disunion did I say? Whether disunion shall approach us, rests not with ourselves, but with our Northern brethren. Forbearance and pusillanimity in the South, may retard, but cannot finally prevent disunion. . . . It is firmness alone, which in the end, will, in my humble view, lead to the regeneration of the liberties and the sovereignties of the States, as secured by the Federal Constitution. . . .[45]

While the Turnbull essays spoke only in part to the issue of the tariff (their primary target was efforts on behalf of colonization of free blacks by some members of Congress), Thomas Cooper was more pointed in his attacks. Cooper was president of South Carolina College, and one of the best-known advocates of states' rights principles in the South. On July 2, 1827, speaking at a huge anti-tariff meeting in Columbia, South Carolina, he sounded an alarm which was heard all over the nation. He began by pointing to the injured interests in the South that resulted from protection:

The planting interest, refusing to become the dupes have at length after a series of successful attacks upon them during the last ten years, become the victims of manufacturing monopoly. The avowed object now is, by means of a drilled and managed majority in congress, permanently to force upon us a system, whose effect will be to sacrifice the south to the north, by converting us into colonies and tributaries—to tax us for their own emolument—to claim the right of disposing of our honest earnings—to forbid us to buy from our most valuable customers—to irritate into retaliation our foreign purchasers, and thus confine our raw materials to the home market—in short to impoverish the planter, and to stretch the purse of the manufacturer.[46]

In his climactic peroration, Cooper stated that, if tariffs remained high:

. . . we shall 'ere long be compelled to calculate the value of our union; and to enquire of what use to us is this most unequal alliance? By which the south has always been the loser, and north always the gainer? Is it worth our while to continue this union of states, where the north demand to be our masters and we are required to be their tributaries? . . . The question . . . is fast approaching to the alternative, of submission or separation.[47]

Cooper's phrase, "calculate the value of our union," electrified the rest of the nation, and forced new recognition of the depths of South Carolina's opposition. Indeed, Cooper's threat was not simply alarmist; it was an accurate reflection of the state of mind of participants in regime conflicts. As Cooper pointed out, when regime parameters change in any substantial way—when, for instance, a group which was once a majority in a political system becomes a minority and loses control over allocations—those participants who feel disadvantaged by those changes may well reassess their participation and decide that their costs under a transformed regime exceed the benefits they receive. "Calculating the value of the union" was a natural and almost inescapable concomitant of what some Southerners perceived to be serious alterations in regime goals.

The belief that the South was no longer an equal beneficiary of the national government's activities was very clear in the protests against the tariff, as exemplified in the following memorial to Congress transmitted in 1827 by the citizens of Richland District, South Carolina:

The duties laid by Congress, of whatever description, are levied in great part on articles purchased by Southern industry and consumed by the South; but these duties are expended almost exclusively for the benefit of other sections of the Union. All of the taxes that support the expenditures of the army, of the navy, of the various fortifications, of roads and canals, in whatever proportion we pay them, return to us no more. All that is taken from us is disposed of elsewhere. We are benefitted in the South by those expenditures in no way that we can perceive and feel. All that we pay is accumulated in defending and improving distant sections of the Union, and the prosperity of the North is built upon the impoverishment of the South. Although we have long submitted without complaint, the inequality and injustice of this state of things is becoming too glaring to remain unnoticed, and the burdens it imposes on us too heavy to be borne in silence any longer.[48]

In addition to the claim that tax revenues were not spent in the South in proportion to the region's contributions to them, Southern spokesmen also argued that the protective tariff hurt their section's economy, based as it was on the production of staple crops for export. For example, in the twelve months ending September 30, 1827, the nation as a whole exported $59.9 million worth of goods; of the total, raw cotton exports represented $29.4 million, tobacco claimed $6.6 million, and rice was worth $2.3 million. In short, those three Southern staple crops represented almost two-thirds of all American exports. Southerners argued that those exports were paying for the country's imports, and that Southern production was therefore the means of exchange for most of the imported merchandise. Since the tariff added to the cost of imports, it diminished the amount which Americans could purchase, and consequently diminished the amount of cotton and other crops foreign nations could buy in exchange. So the protective tariff aided the Northern manufacturers, the planters agreed, but only at the cost of considerable damage to Southern agricultural trade.[49] While the economic validity of these arguments was suspect, their emotional impact was substantial, especially when translated by practiced orators like George McDuffie into such evocative rhetoric as his "forty-bale theory," which suggested that, out of every hundred bales of cotton harvested for export, the tariff stole forty through its effects on trade.[50]

Lurking behind all of these arguments was the very real fear that the national government, set free from the bounds of strict construction, could impose other injurious policies on the new Southern minority, and that no constitutional mechanism existed for defense against such majoritarian tyranny. The tariff demonstrated that the North and West would ignore Southern claims of grave injury if the policy in question benefited them sufficiently. What was to stop them from abolishing slavery if they chose to?

With a growing sense of helplessness, the South made another attempt to stave off protection in Congress. Now that the impetus of the Harrisburg convention was behind them, protectionists hoped to get favorable action in Congress during the 1827–28 session. Indeed, a bill for increased duties was reported out of the Committee on Manufactures in January 1828. But the bill was not strong enough for the chairman of the committee, Rollin Mallary, who suggested further amendments to bring it into line with the recommendations of the manufacturers and their allies at Harrisburg.

The committee bill asked increased duties on woolens, but reduced those tariffs from the prohibitory level of the Harrisburg demands. In addition, the bill asked for a duty on raw wool high enough to raise its price to domestic manufacturers, and for new duties on iron, hemp, and molasses, all of which would infuriate New England shipowners, merchants, and distillers. In committee, the bill had been written primarily by Silas Wright, a product of Van Buren's Albany Regency and the New York Senator's close ally. And most historians agree that Van Buren put the bill forward with full expectation that it would not pass.[51] The gambit was devious and risky, but the stakes were high:

> Any tariff bill would be objectionable to the South. This one was carefully and deliberately framed to be objectionable to New England also. Thus Jackson's Pennsylvania, New York, and Ohio followers could vote for it, and Southern Jacksonians could oppose. The bill would be defeated by New England to the great damage of the [Adams] administration; the South would be satisfied; and Jackson would remain on both sides of the question.[52]

The administration forces in the House were well aware of the Jacksonian strategy. Representative John Bailey of Massachusetts, who often reflected Adams' view, quickly understood that the administration was trapped. In a note to a friend, he stated that the tariff bill "was framed precisely to defeat itself, as it will if not amended as Mallary had proposed," and he charged that the committee bill "was engendered between the avowed anti-tariff men of the South, and the *professed* tariff Jackson men of the middle states, and framed most pointedly so as to bear heavily and injuriously on New England, in the hope that it would thus be defected." [53] His colleague from Massachusetts, Isaac Bates, complained with barely disguised bitterness in a speech in the House:

> Without calling into question the motives of the committee, I say that if this bill had been formed for the express purpose of defeating the object in view; if the committee had called a council and taken advice on how to frame a bill that could not pass this House, or, if it could, that should afford no relief to the manufacturer or wool grower, they could not have framed one better fitted for the purpose than this bill is. [54]

But the sucess of this strategy depended on defeating any amendments that might make it more palatable to the New England delegation. On Mallary's amendment to bring the bill into conformance with the recommendations of the Harrisburg convention, the opposition coalition held, and the amendment was defeated by a vote of 114 to 80. By a much narrower vote, the House also rejected another Mallary amendment to revise the wool duties, and beat back an attempt to reduce the duty on molasses, which New England found so annoying. The only amendment that did pass in the House was a reduction in the specific duty on raw wool from 7¢ to 4¢; but the valorem duty remained at 40 percent. Although they could defeat the bill's amendments, the anti-tariff forces could not turn back an increased tariff. By a vote of 105 to 94, the bill finally passed the House. As expected, Jacksonians from New York, Pennsylvania, and Ohio had to vote for it, and the South held firm, with only Kentucky and a few representatives from western Virginia voting for the tariff. Yet bad as they thought the bill was, administration forces under Clay's direction voted for the bill, and they were able to convince 11 members from New England, who provided the winning margin.

After the bill's passage and before it was sent to the Senate, an attempt was made to make its protectionist character more explicit in hopes of expediting a court test on its constitutionality. When the bill's title was discussed, Representative Wilde of Georgia therefore proposed that the House add the phrase "and for the encouragement of manufactures," in order to show its intent more clearly. Drayton of South Carolina suggested adding "for the purposes of increasing the profits of certain manufactures." Hodges of Massachusetts, whose delegation had voted 11 to 2 against the bill, wanted to call it a bill "to transfer the capital and industry of the New England States to other states in the Union." John Randolph of Virginia, with his customary skill at invective, wanted it labeled "a bill to plunder nearly one half of the Union, for the benefit of the residue." None of the proposals were carried.[55]

In the Senate, the anti-tariff strategy fell apart. The Committee on Manufactures voted out the bill with fourteen amendments designed to reestablish the Harrisburg proposals, and seven of those amendments were accepted by the Senate, giving the New Englanders adequate excuse to vote for the measure. On five of those amendments, the vote was 24 to 22, and Van Buren's own vote in favor of those revisions was, therefore, critical. On one, no roll was called. On the seventh, the vote was 25 to 21, with both Van Buren and John Eaton, Senator from Tennessee and close friend of Jackson, voting in favor. On May 13, the bill was passed by a vote of 26 to 21. Those supporting it included Benton of Missouri and Rowan of Kentucky, who could not oppose the declared will of their states; Eaton of Tennessee; and Van Buren of New York, who had "procured the passage of a resolution by the New York legislature instructing him to vote for the tariff of 1828, and thus relieved himself of responsibility for his vote." [56] Daniel Webster agonized over the bill, which still contained some duties painful to New Englanders, but he believed it would benefit his constituents and voted for it, bringing with him a majority of the New England delegation. What the South and New England came to call the "Tariff of Abominations" had passed.

Jackson's political managers were satisfied with the result. They had voted in favor of the tariff and had thus destroyed its usefulness to Clay as a campaign issue. But members from the South saw the protectionist votes by Van Buren and Eaton in the Senate as breaches of faith, and resented them bitterly. They had made a last attempt to marshal an anti-tariff majority in the legislature, using a dangerously risky strategy, and they had failed. Although the tariff was painful to New England, Southerners felt more than pain; they believed themselves to be tyrannized. The members of Congress from South Carolina, still the forward point of anti-tariff resistance, met after the vote at Senator Hayne's Washington home to discuss further action. They talked about alternatives, some of which the administration press later suggested were "treasonable," made no firm decisions, and returned home to organize in South Carolina.

Throughout the summer, in districts, parishes, and towns, mass meetings were held to denounce the tariff. At a rally in Edgefield in July 26, the tariff of 1828 was compared to the Stamp Act of 1765, and committees of correspondence were formed to plan resistance of some sort. And at Pendelton, Calhoun toasted:

"The Congress of '76—They taught the world how oppression could be resisted, may the lesson teach rulers that their only safety is in justice and moderation." [57]

But no consensus on any single course of action appeared. Senator William Smith and Congressman William Martin proposed that the South Carolina legislature enact a prohibitive excise tax on Northern goods, and George McDuffie pushed that movement forward in a famous speech in the state capital during which he tore off his coat of Northern broadcloth. Other politicians and planters began appearing dressed in Southern homespun, but nonimportation was a small-bore weapon. [58] To radical South Carolinians, the only step that made sense was open resistance to the law. Robert Barnwell Rhett, the most militant of the Southerners, proposed in June 1828 that an immediate session of the state legislature be called, and that South Carolina begin to "resist. . . . Not secretly, as timid thieves of skulking Smugglers—not in companies and associations, like money chafferers or stock jobbers—not separately & individually, as if this were ours and not our Country's cause—but openly, fairly, fearlessly and unitedly." [59] Most observers read this as a call to secession.

More moderate politicians still hoped that milder tactics would suffice. Some believed that Jackson's election might bring tariff relief. Others, like Calhoun, concocted plans to split the alliance of North and West, and to establish instead a coalition between the South and the West, the two great agricultural sections of the country. In return for Western support of tariff reductions, the South would support proposals for more liberal land policies in the West. But before they felt free to play out these alternatives, the politicians had to reestablish closer control over events in South Carolina.

In a letter to Monroe in July 1828, Calhoun said that he was worried by the discontent he saw around him in the South, and by the structural deficiencies that prevented the regime from dealing with that discontent:

. . . the system pushed to the present extreme acts most unequally in its pressure on the several parts, which has of necessity a most pernicious tendancy on the feelings of the oppressed portions. I greatly fear, that the weak part of our system will be found to consist in the fact that in a country of such vast extent and diversity of interest, many of the laws will be found to act very unequally, and that some portions of the country may be enriched by legislation at the expense of others. It seems to me that we have no other check against abuses, but such as grow out of responsibility, or elections, and while this is an effectual check, where the law acts equally on all, it is none in the case of the unequal action to which I refer. One thing seems to me certain, that the system is getting wrong and if a speedy and effective remedy be not applied a shock at no long interval may be expected.

But Calhoun also believed, as he told Monroe, that "the attachment to the Union remains unshaken with the great body of citizens," and privately he was certain that a "speedy and effective remedy" was indeed at hand that would provide "an effectual check" and still maintain the attachment to the Union of most of the population.[60] The remedy, of course, was nullification, which Calhoun had embraced intellectually in 1827, even though he did not publicly declare himself for it until 1831. But whatever his public stance, Calhoun saw nullification as a middle course, conceivable under the constitutional framework of the existing regime, but radical enough as an active course of resistance to slow the rush towards secession. So when he was asked in the fall of 1828 to write a statement of the doctrine for the South Carolina legislature, he agreed on condition that his authorship remain secret. The result was the *South Carolina Exposition and Protest,* a classic statement on the issue.[61]

Calhoun put forward briefly the now conventional protest that protection was unconstitutional because it was nowhere explicit in the charter document. But that narrow argument was made in only two pages, and the rest of the sixty-page pamphlet analyzed what Calhoun believed to be the deeper regime issues, and offered a lucid treatment of his remedy—nullification. Calhoun rehearsed the arguments about how the South suffered real economic costs in trade limitations and in higher prices for its own purchases of finished products, an issue of special concern for slave owners who had to buy clothing and other equipment for their workers. And because the Southern economy was so dependent upon the export of staple products, he warned of the long-term dangers of protection's effect on trade relations with England:

We already see indications of the commencement of a commercial warfare, the termination of which no one can conjecture,—though our fate may easily be. The last remains of our great and once flourishing agriculture must be annihilated in the conflict. . . .

Forced to abandon our ancient and favorite pursuit, to which our soil, climate, habits, and peculiar labor are adapted, at immense sacrifice of property, we would be compelled, without capital, experience, or skill, and with a population untried in such pursuits, to attempt to become the rivals instead of the customers of the manufacturing States.[62]

Southerners were now "the serfs of the system,—out of whose labor is used, not only the money paid into the Treasury, but the funds out of which are drawn the rich rewards of the manufacturers." [63] That new subordinate status was proof that a gross and unwarranted transformation of regime had taken place without the consent of the South.

In years to come, Calhoun would see this redistribution of power as the fundamental cause of the struggle between North and South. In 1850, during the legislative debate on Clay's compromise proposals for resolving the dispute over the boundaries of slavery, Calhoun wondered aloud what had brought about this great crisis which seemed to endanger the Union. Calhoun believed that the "great and primary cause" was that "the equilibrium between the two sections, as it stood when the Constitution was ratified," had been destroyed. While at one time each section had sufficient political means to defend itself against "the agressions of the other, . . . now one section has the exclusive power of controlling the Government. . . ." Calhoun went on to state that that balance had not disappeared naturally, but that its destruction was effected by the North through exclusion of the South from the common territory of the West, through tariff laws which hindered Southern progress, and through a remorseless concentration of power in the central government.[64]

In 1828, Calhoun still had hope that the crucial balance could be maintained. He recognized the difficulty of convincing the North to relinquish its tariff advantage in the face of only mild threats from the South. "For the present, all was flourishing," he conceded, and wondered aloud why the North "would forgo practical gains in the present for hypothetical losses in the future?" [65] He nonetheless attempted to make the nature of those losses plain. In a stunning passage that foreshadowed Marx's class analysis, Calhoun argued that the protective tariff would someday destroy the North as well as the South by creating an American proletariat: *

* This passage was a bit strong for the South Carolina legislature, and they edited it out of the version of the *Exposition* they printed and distributed.

No system can be more efficient to rear up a moneyed aristocracy. Its tendency is, to make the poor poorer, and rich richer. Heretofore, in our country, this tendency has displayed itself principally in its effects, as regards the different sections,—but the time will come when it will produce the same results between the several classes in the manufacturing States. After we are exhausted, the contest will be between the capitalists and operatives; for into these two classes must, ultimately, divide society. The issue of the struggle here must be the same as it has been in Europe. Under the operation of the system, wages must sink more rapidly than the prices of the necessaries of life, until the operatives will be reduced to the lowest point,—when the portion of the products of their labor left to them will be barely sufficient to preserve existence.[66]

But the fear of class warfare at some indistinct time in the future would not persuade manufacturers to abandon protection. Some more immediate threat was required—one with impact dramatic enough to frighten the North, yet sufficiently restrained so that secession, the ultimate danger to the Union, could be held at bay. As the struggle over the tariff of 1828 had demonstrated, existing remedies were simply inadequate;

But if it be supposed that, from diversity of interests in the several classes and sections of the country, the laws act differently, so that the same law, though couched in general terms and apparently fair, shall, in reality, transfer the power and property of one class or section to another,—in such a case, responsibility to constituents, which is but the means of enforcing fidelity of representatives to them, must prove wholly insufficient to preserve the purity of public agents, or the liberty of the country. It would, in fact, fall short of the evil. The disease would be in the community itself,—in the constituents, and not their representatives. The opposing interests of the community would engender, necessarily, opposing hostile parties,—organized on this very diversity of interests,—the stronger of which, if the Government provided no efficient check, would exercise unlimited and unrestrained power over the weaker. The relationship of equality between the parts of the community, established by the Constitution, would be destroyed and in its place there would be substituted the relation of sovereign and subject, between the stronger and weaker interests, in its most odious and oppressive form.[67]

In short, because the real political basis of the regime had been altered, with subordination replacing sectional equality, legislative and electoral action could no longer redress the balance.

A new mechanism was required, a new set of processes that would preserve the power of minorities to restrain alterations of the regime that might damage their interests, and the answer was nullification. Calhoun's premise was that constitution-making and law-making were not and could not be the same process. While the national government could make laws as prescribed under the Constitution, it could not be itself the judge of the limits of the Constitution, either in its legislature or through the Supreme Court. If the national government decided the constitutional validity of its own actions, there would be no effective boundaries to its power. In the last resort, Calhoun argued, the constitutional power to determine the limits of the regime's authority must rest elsewhere, and the most reasonable place to find that absolute sovereignty was in the states. After all, it was the states in convention that ratified the Constitution, and so the states in conventions must maintain the final right to interpret that compact.

Calhoun proposed that a single state, through a convention established by its legislature, could nullify a federal law and therefore prevent its operation within the state's boundaries. Faced with that definitive judgment as to the constitutionality of its action, the national government could either repeal the law, or present an amendment to the Constitution. If three-quarters of the states agreed to the amendment, the national government's powers would be legitimately expanded. It was, Calhoun pointed out, insufficient to argue that a state could itself propose an amendment to halt some action of the national government:

> The disease is, that a majority of the States, through the General Government, by construction, usurp powers not delegated, and by their exercise, increase their wealth and authority at the expense of the minority. How absurd, then, to expect the injured States to attempt a remedy by proposing an amendment to be ratified by three fourths of the States, when by supposition there is a majority opposed to them? [68]

Without the power of state interposition, "the will of the majority, under the agency of construction, would be substituted, with unlimited and supreme power." If however, the possibility of state nullification exists, the system works perfectly:

> . . . all controversies between the States and General Government would be adjusted, and the Constitution gradually acquire all the perfection of which it is susceptible. It is thus that the *creating* be-

comes the *preserving* power; and we may rest assured it is no less true in politics than in theology, that the power which creates can alone preserve,—and that preservation is perpetual creation. Such will be the operation and effect of State interposition.[69]

The Virginia and Kentucky Resolutions had hinted at the possibility of state action against the Alien and Sedition Acts, and therefore provided some weak precedent for nullification. But because men like McDuffie attacked state interposition as nothing more than "a sugar-coated version of secession," [70] Calhoun was careful to point out that nullification was in fact a fundamentally conservative remedy, and was not subject to abuse by the masses:

> . . . the checking or veto power never has, in any country, or under any institution, been lodged where it was less liable to abuse. The great number, by whom it must be exercised, of the people in a State,—the solemnity of the mode,—a Convention especially called for the purpose, and representing the State in her highest capacity,— the delay,—the deliberation,—are all calculated to allay excitement,—to impress on the people a deep and solemn tone, highly favorable to calm investigation and decision. . . . So powerful, in fact, are these difficulties, that nothing but truth and a deep sense of oppression on the part of the people of the State, will ever sustain the exercise of the power. . . .[71]

When the South Carolina legislature ordered the printing of 5,000 copies of the *Exposition*, it embellished them with a set of resolutions entitled "PROTEST." Although Calhoun himself had barely mentioned slavery, the last of those resolutions made it evident that the survivial of that institution lay near the heart of the tariff issue for Southerners:

> 8th. Finally, because South Carolina, from her climate, situation, and peculiar institutions, is, and must ever continue to be, wholly dependent upon agriculture and commerce, not only for her prosperity, but for her very existence as a State—because the valuable products of her soil—the blessings by which Divine Providence seems to have designed to compensate for the great disadvantages under which she suffers in other respects—are among the very few that can be cultivated with any profit by slave labor—and if, by the loss of her foreign commerce, these products should be confined to an inadequate market, the fate of this fertile State would be poverty and utter desolation; her citizens, in despair, would emigrate to more fortunate

regions, and the whole frame and constitution of her civil polity be impaired and deranged, if not dissolved entirely.[72]

The struggle, as South Carolina had framed it, was for the survival of the whole of Southern civilization, dependent as it was on slave labor and plantation agriculture. As Barrington Moore suggested in his essay on the root causes of the Civil War:

> Essentially we are asking whether the institutional requirement for operating a plantation economy based on slavery clashed seriously at any point with the corresponding requirements for operating a capitalist industrial society. . . . It should . . . be clear that the requirements or structural imperatives for plantation slavery and early industrial capitalism extend far beyond economic arrangements as such and certainly into the area of social institutions. Slave societies do not have the same political forms as those based on free labor.[73]

In the terms favored in this essay, survival of a slave society required a very different kind of political regime than the North's industrializing society. The ideological bases of authority were different, for instance. John Randolph had once said that "the South had accepted the Union on the assumption that the power of government would remain in the hands of the landed classes, who alone have that understanding of tradition, without which no society can be healthy." [74] Moore agreed with Randolph's assessment of the ideological needs of the South:

> Southern society was based firmly on hereditary status as the basis of human worth. With the West, the North, though still in the process of change, was still committed to notions of equal opportunity. In both, the ideals were reflections of economic arrangements that gave them much of their appeal and force. Within the same political unit, it was, I think inherently impossible to establish political and social institutions that would satisfy both.[75]

Because the South and the North were very different societies, they needed different things from the national political regime. They needed different ideological justifications for state authority. They needed different allocative policies: the tariff and internal improvements were of little use to the South in the maintenance of its social order, but were costly in taxes. They needed different levels of coercion: the South needed strict laws and enforcement systems to maintain its labor-repressive agriculture, while the North needed the rhetoric and climate of rela-

tive freedom to match its free-market economy. The fight over these different regime requirements finally culminated in the Civil War, but its
outlines can be discerned in the tariff struggles thirty years before.

In his statement on nullification, Calhoun had attempted to provide
quasi-constitutional parameters for the struggle against the tariff, and he
was probably pleased to see that, when the South Carolina legislature
reconvened in November 1828, even its most radical members were satisfied to push for a nullification convention. But the nullifiers in the legislature were divided among themselves, and the conservatives cleverly exploited those divisions and defeated the call for a convention. The
legislature also refused to adopt the *Exposition*, although it paid for its
printing and distribution and passed the strong set of resolutions referred
to above. Calhoun, while disturbed at the legislature's editorial emenda-
tions, was not unhappy with the delay. He wanted to see what the Jackson administration would do about the tariff, and saw some hope for
separating the West from the North and rebuilding an anti-tariff majority
in the Congress. Finally, he still nurtured presidential ambitions of his
own, which might be destroyed by radical action in his home state.[76]

But when the first of Jackson's annual messages to Congress was delivered in December 1828, it offered the South little hope. Jackson said that
the tariff had proved less beneficial than expected to manufacturers and
less harmful to planters than feared, and he recommended reductions
only on articles such as tea and coffee, which were not in direct competition with domestic products. George McDuffie, now chairman of the
House Ways and Means Committee, had bolder plans, and he quickly reported out a bill to reduce most of the 1824 and 1828 rates that the South
found so abhorent. To his great dismay, the House promptly voted by the
sizable margin of 107 to 79 to table his bill without debate, and the only
tariff reductions passed during that session of Congress were cuts in the
levies on salt, tea, coffee, cocoa, and molasses. While the reduction in the
molasses tax did away with one of the "abominations" that had hurt New
England most, the duties that concerned the South most strongly—the
ones on iron, cottons, and woolens—remained unchanged.

In that same session, a dramatic but unsuccessful attempt was made by
Southern representatives to pry Western votes loose from their customary
support of the tariff. The historic Hayne–Webster debates began with a
resolution offered in the Senate by Samuel Foote of Connecticut, suggesting that the Congress investigate possible limitations on the sale of public

lands. Thomas Hart Benton, one of the West's most eloquent spokesmen, complained that New England and the other manufacturing states wanted to stop the settlement of the West, and thereby maintain a large pool of cheap labor for their factories. Looking to the South for support, Benton suggested that restrictions on land sales would provide the same kind of indirect subsidy to manufacturing as the tariff, and he argued that both policies together constituted "a most complex scheme of injustice, which taxes the South to injure the West, to pauperize the poor of the North." [77]

Robert Y. Hayne, Senator from South Carolina, rose to offer sympathy and support, and to propose a combined program of low tariffs and low land prices. The Treasury had projected that the national debt would be fully retired within four years. Hayne suggested that at that time the federal government should sell its lands to the states for nominal sums, and should leave the states free to dispose of them as they pleased.

Protectionists recognized the dangers implicit in a West–South alliance, and they moved to counterattack, with Daniel Webster carrying the major burden of the battle. His first reply to Hayne was not, in fact, a continuation of the discussion on land policy, but rather a successful attempt to change the grounds of debate. He attacked the South in general, and South Carolina in particular, for changing its policies from early support of the tariff to what he believed was menacing opposition. "I know that there are some persons in the part of the country from which the honorable member comes, who habitually speak of the Union in terms of indifference, or even disparagement. . . . They significantly declare, that it is time to calculate the value of the Union." [78]

As intended, Webster provoked a debate over states rights and national supremacy. Hayne followed with a harsh speech castigating New England and Federalism, quoting Webster's own anti-tariff speech of 1824, and defending the doctrine of nullification as South Carolina's effort on behalf of "the preservation of the Union, by the only means by which she believes it can be preserved—a firm, manly, and steady resistance against usurpation." [79]

In Webster's second reply, he continued his attack on disunionists with a heady appeal to patriotism that has been a standby of Fourth of July orators ever since. He defended New England against charges that its activities had ever offered any precedent for disunion, and concluded with a famous peroration:

When my eyes shall be turned to behold, for the last time, the sun in heaven, may I not see him shining on the broken and dishonored fragments of a once glorious Union. . . . Let their last feeble and lingering glance, rather, behold the gorgeous ensign of the republic blazing on all its ample folds, as they float over the sea and over the land . . . . Liberty and Union, now and forever, one and insepara- ble.[80]

By suggesting that the South was flirting with treason, Webster's patri- otic rhetoric had helped to head off the West–South alliance. Moreover, the debates revealed the difficult and somewhat contradictory position in which the Southern moderates now found themselves. William Freehling, an historian of the nullification crisis, puts it thus:

The Hayne–Webster debates reveal the nullifiers at the crossroads. By continuing to work hopefully within the old system of shifting ma- jority coalitions, as in Hayne's first oration, Calhounites obscured the necessity for immediate nullification. By supporting nullification, as in Hayne's second oration, Calhounites weakened the possibility of achieving the victory within the majoritarian tradition.[81]

Quickly enough, other events indicated that the attempt to capture the national government and thereby reform tariff policies would be unsuc- cessful. Calhoun, who as Jackson's Vice-President was the key to Southern influence in the new administration, was no longer in the President's favor. Under Mrs. Calhoun's leadership, the cabinet wives had ostracized the new spouse of John Eaton, Jackson's close friend and Secretary of War. Eaton eventually resigned, and Jackson believed that Calhoun was in part to blame. The President had also discovered that Calhoun had misrepresented his position in an earlier dispute over Jackson's conduct during the Seminole War. Finally, Jackson publically and dramatically rebuked Calhoun and the nullifiers at the Jefferson Day dinner of 1830, an occasion obstensibly dedicated to party unity.

As the Calhoun faction lost influence in Washington, the nullifiers gained ground in South Carolina politics. They won the 1830 state legisla- tive elections, and were strong enough to pass a series of resolutions which proclaimed that, in spite of their attachment to the Union, action was necessary to restrain the national government from its movement toward absolutism. They stated as well that the tariff was a violation of the constitutional compact between the states, and should be stopped by interposition if no other remedy sufficed. But the most important resolution, which called for a state convention, failed to muster the required two-thirds vote in either the state senate or the lower house, and did not pass.

The direct threat to slavery was also growing. In 1830, a bill was introduced on behalf of the American Colonization Society calling for federal contributions toward the removal of free blacks to Africa. Most of the South saw this as the beginnings of a scheme to excite the slaves, regulate the institutions of slavery, and eventually abolish it altogether. Their fears were not lessened by the appearance on New Year's Day 1831 of William Lloyd Garrison's militant abolitionist journal, the *Liberator*. And in the summer of 1831, Nat Turner led a brief but bloody slave rebellion in Virginia that sent shivers through the white South.

In March 1831, however, Calhoun still had hopes that the West and the South could come together to beat down the tariff, and to elect him President. But George McDuffie, in a passionate speech in Charleston, complained that conventionally moderate political action was unworthy of the revolutionary heritage of the citizens of South Carolina. He scoffed at those who unthinkingly supported the authority of the Union, stated that "the Union, as the majority have made it, is a foul monster," and reminded his listeners of the heroic activism of their ancestors:

> They commenced the revolution that secured our liberty, when their oppressions were not one hundredth part as grievous as ours. . . . With halters around their necks, and the stigma of treason on their foreheads, nobly disdaining to count the costs of the contest, which, though they should perish, was to secure liberty to their posterity, they fearlessly encountered the gigantic power of a mighty nation. And with this glorious example before us, shall we basely surrender the inheritance of our children . . . ?" [82]

Within South Carolina, a unionist faction opposed nullification altogether, and its leaders organized an Independence Day celebration in Charleston which featured a supportive letter from President Jackson himself. Jackson equated nullification with secession, labeled it an unacceptable and unconstitutional means of redress, and promised firm action to hold the Union together:

> Every enlightened citizen must know, that a separation, could it be effected, would begin with civil discord, and end in colonial depen-

dence on a foreign power, and obliteration from the list of nations. But he should also see that high and sacred duties which must and will, at all hazards, be performed, present an insurmountable barrier to the success of any plan of disorganization, by whatever patriotic name it may be decorated, or whatever high feelings may be arrayed for its support. . . .[83]

As their opponents tried to identify nullification with radicalism, the Calhounites tried again to represent the doctrine as peaceful and constitutional. In a Fourth of July speech, Senator Hayne reviewed the moderate arguments in favor of nullification. A month later, Calhoun himself finally abandoned his public silence of the issue. In the Fort Hill address, named for his South Carolina estate, Calhoun openly restated the logic of nullification as he had laid it out anonymously in the *Exposition*. In doing so, of course, he put his enormous personal prestige behind the doctrine. As Calhoun's biographer put it: "The Fort Hill Address was a very important document, for Calhoun and for the nation. The prestige and distinction of its author meant that nullification must thereafter be taken seriously, by its opponents as well as its friends. The subject was presented in the best possible light, under the highest possible auspices, and it could not be ignored." [84]

Calhoun's supporters distributed 3,000 copies of the address throughout the state, along with 1,000 copies of Hayne's speech. With Calhoun finally pushed from the middle of the road, the nullifiers made relatively rapid progress in South Carolina. James Hamilton Jr. helped organize associations to campaign for the doctrine, and tracts and pamphlets were distributed throughout the state. The aim was to elect enough sympathizers to the state legislature to guarantee a nullification convention.

On the national level, too, the nullification campaign seemed to be having some impact. In December 1831, Jackson's message to Congress was moderate and conciliatory in its tone. He predicted that the debt would be paid off within a year, and proposed tariff modifications at that time: "A modification of the tariff, which shall produce a reduction of our revenue to the wants of the government, and an adjustment of the duties on imports with a view to equal justice in relation to all our national interests . . . is deemed to be one of the principal objects which demand the consideration of the present congress." [85]

But when Secretary of the Treasury Louis McLane proposed reductions, he said nothing about those items of greatest importance to the South (iron, hemp, wool and woolens). Another path seemed closed when Henry Clay decided that the bank charter, not the tariff, would be the main issue in the coming election, since the South could no longer trade support for his presidential bid for promises of future tariff relief. Nor could they accede to Jackson's tariff proposals, because reductions in and of themselves were not enough for the South. They were fighting for an interpretation of the Constitution that would help them defend slavery; to that end, they insisted either that the state nullify the tariff law, or that the national government act in clearly stated response to South Carolina's demands.[86] The federal government had to demonstrate that it was still responsive to Southern needs, or South Carolina would create a tool to guarantee that responsiveness. So Calhoun notified McLane that his proposals were inadequate, and advised the nullifiers in South Carolina to continue their work.

In early 1832, Andrew Jackson unwittingly gave his Southern opponents grounds to hope that nullification might be accomplished without resistance from the presidency. In *Worchester v. Georgia*,[87] the Supreme Court denied the legal authority of the State of Georgia within the boundaries of Cherokee territories. But both Georgia and the President ignored the ruling, which occasioned Jackson's famous (if possibly apocryphal) statement: "John Marshall has made his decision; now let him enforce it." Georgia continued its encroachment on Indian territory, nullifying Marshall's decision in fact, even if Georgians produced no new constitutional arguments in support of their action.[88]

In January 1832, Henry Clay reopened the tariff debate in Congress by introducing into the Senate a resolution to abolish duties on foreign articles which did not directly compete with domestic manufactures. At the same time, he proposed prohibitive taxes on items which were to be protected, such as distilled spirits. Although Clay hoped that the plan for reductions might bring his presidential bid some support from the South, his scheme did little to decrease the inequalities which disturbed the South and did nothing to break down the principle of protection, which was by now all-important to the nullifiers. When the resolution came up for debate, Hayne moved to amend it to reduce the tariff to the level necessary to sustain the government's needs for revenues, and to phase out protective tariffs over some reasonable period of time, so that American manufacturers could prepare for competition. But Clay rejected that compromise; and, with support from New England and the Northwest, Clay's resolution passed and became the basis for a Senate bill on the tariff.

The House Committee on Manufactures was under the chairmanship of John Quincy Adams, who was anxious to preserve protection but believed as well that some tariff reductions were necessary to mollify the South. Adams introduced his own bill, which removed most of the 1828 "abominations," and reduced nonprotective schedules across the board. But it did little to change most protective duties, and administration supporters beat back amendments designed to conciliate the South. The Adams bill passed the House on June 28, by a wide margin of 132 to 65, with the South still in opposition, and passed the Senate on July 9, by a vote of 32 to 16.

The tariff of 1832 abolished the "minimum" system for evaluating woolen goods, which had been subject to large-scale evasion by shippers. The average level of all duties was reduced from 41 percent to 33 percent, and most rates were set back to the level of the 1824 tariff. From the protectionist point of view, the only industry that suffered severely was the woolens manufacturers, but both the administration and the National Republicans loudly applauded the concessions their act made, and argued that the bill represented a final settlement of the tariff problem.

South Carolina was not convinced, as it proved in the legislative elections in the fall of 1832. The campaign for those offices was fiercely fought. Each party adopted emblems: the Nullifiers wore blue cockades and palmetto buttons, the Unionists chose American eagles. And they fought with each other, in duels, in street brawls, and at huge and noisy rallies. A recent historian of the nullification controversy suggests that it was difficult to understand how the tariff alone could so energize South Carolina politics, and he looks for an explanation to the deeper and more emotional issue of slavery. As George McDuffie warned his countrymen:

> Any course of measures which shall hasten the abolition of slavery by destroying the value of slave labor, will bring upon the southern States the greatest political calamity with which they can be afflicted. . . . It is the clear and distinct perception of the irresistable tendency of this protecting system to precipitate upon us this great moral and political catastrophe, that has animated me to raise my warning voice, that my fellow citizens may foresee and foreseeing, avoid the destiny that would otherwise befall them.

John C. Calhoun made the same point in a letter to a friend:

I consider the Tariff, just as the occasion, rather than the real cause
of the present unhappy state of things. The truth can no longer be
disguised, that the peculiar domestick institutions of the Southern
States, and the consequent direction which that and her soil and
climate have given to her industry, has placed them in regard to taxation and appropriation in opposite relation to the majority of the
Union; against the dangers of which, if there be no protective power
in the reserved rights of the states, they must in the end be forced to
rebel, or submit to have . . . their domestick institutions exhausted
by Colonization and other schemes, and themselves & their children
reduced to wretchedness. Thus situated, the denial of the right of the
state to interfere constitutionally in the last resort, more alarms the
thinking than all other causes.[89]

Disturbed by the passion the struggle was eliciting in his neighbors,
Calhoun wrote a public letter to Governor James Hamilton Jr. shortly
after election day, reminding the voters that nullification was meant to be
a conservative, peaceful, and constitutional mode of redress.[90] At the
same time, he wrote to a friend that the cause of nullification would
triumph in the election: ". . . but any movement will be made with the
view of preserving the Union. The end aimed at will be a general convention of all the States, in order to adjust all constitutional differences, and
thus restore general harmony. We have run nearly fifty years on the first
tack. It is a wonderful run; but it is time to bring up the reckoning, in
order to take a fresh departure." [91]

The Nullifiers did win, with a popular majority of some 6,000 out of
about 40,000 votes cast; they captured over two-thirds of the seats in the
assembly, and nearly three-fourths of the state senate. When the legislative elections were concluded, Governor Hamilton quickly called a special
session of the new legislature. Within three days a bill was passed establishing elections for delegates to a nullification convention. At the same
time, South Carolina's presidential electors decided to express their dis-
satisfaction with the choice between Jackson and Clay by casting the
state's eleven electoral votes for the peculiar ticket of John Floyd, Governor of Virginia, and Henry Lee, a free-trade pamphleteer from Massachusetts.

Some Unionists refused to participate at all in the balloting, and thus most of the delegates elected to the convention were Nullifiers. But within the ranks of the Nullifiers, those extremists who saw nullification as nothing more than a first step to secession opposed the moderates who, following Calhoun, saw it as the only way to prevent disunion. They clashed on such issues as the date when the proposed ordinance would take effect (they compromised on February 1, 1833) and the question of secession (the subcommittee writing the ordinance chose to insert an unqualified declaration that the state would secede if coercion was used against it by the national government).[92]

In essays in support of the ordinance passed by the Convention, the Nullifiers stated their terms for a settlement—a tariff with equal duties on protected and unprotected items, and with a overall rate of no more than 12 percent. The ordinance itself declared that the tariffs of 1828 and 1832 were unconstitutional and null and void within the state of South Carolina. It declared that "we will consider the passage by Congress of any act authorizing the employment of military or naval force against the State of South Carolina . . . as inconsistent with the longer continuance of South Carolina in the Union." [93] Finally, to ensure its enforcement, the ordinance included provisions requiring all state officers elected after the convention to take test oaths in support of nullification.

While the state's political elite was gathered in Columbia, some other important decisions were made. At a party caucus called just after the convention, Robert Hayne agreed to give up his seat in the Senate and become governor, so that his calm demeanor and enormous prestige could be used to manage the struggle at home. And since Calhoun's open support of nullification made his status as Andrew Jackson's Vice-President thoroughly incongruous, Calhoun agreed to resign that post and take Hayne's seat in the Senate.

Calhoun and the other Nullifiers had hoped for support from other Southern states, but were badly disappointed. Every Southern legislature proclaimed its abhorrence of nullification: Alabama said it was "alarming," and "unsound in theory and dangerous in practice"; Georgia complained that the "mischievous policy" was "rash and revolutionary"; and Mississippi stated that South Carolina had acted with "reckless precipitancy." [94]

On the other hand, the first response from Washington—Jackson's annual message on December 4—was mild and moderate on the issue of the tariff. The President grumbled about the difficulties "in one quarter of the

United States" which threatened the execution of the revenue laws, and might "endanger the Integrity of the Union"; but he also stated that, since the national debt had been paid, revenues should be reduced in some way so as to "remove those burdens which shall be found to fall unequally" on any of the great interests of the nation. Jackson recommended that "the whole scheme of duties be reduced to the revenue standard as soon as a just regard to the faith of the government and the preservation of the large capital invested in establishments of domestic industry will permit," noting that the tariff tended "to beget in the minds of a large portion of our countrymen a spirit of discontent and jealousy dangerous to the stability of the Union." [95] As if to reinforce Jackson's conciliatory tone, his administration's newspaper, the Washington *Globe*, called for the reduction of the tariff to "the standards of a safe and prudent, moderate but adequate revenue—not because that measure is demanded by menaces; but because it is just in itself, and is due to the feelings of an important section of the country." [96]

But on December 10, Jackson spoke directly to the issue of state interposition, and he was no longer conciliatory. In a resounding proclamation, he spoke out against nullification as a political remedy:

> I consider . . . the power to annul a law of the United States, assumed by one State, *incompatible with the existence of the Union, contradicted expressly by the letter of the Constitution, unauthorized by its spirit, inconsistent with every principle on which it was founded, and destructive of the great object for which it was formed.*

He lumped together nullification and secession, and denounced them both angrily:

> . . . each State, having expressly parted with so many powers as to constitute, jointly with the other States, a single nation, cannot, from that period, possess any right to secede, because secession does not break a league, but destroys the unity of a nation. . . . Secession, like any other revolutionary act, may be morally justified by the extremity of oppression; but to call it a constitutional right is confounding the meaning of terms, and can only be done through gross error, or to deceive those who are willing to assert a right, but would pause before they made a revolution or incur the penalties consequent on a failure.

Jackson reminded his readers that he was bound by his oath of office to execute the laws of the United States, admonished the citizens of South Carolina to show better sense, and concluded with a warning:

> Disunion by armed force is *treason*. Are you really ready to incur its guilt? If you are, on the heads of the instigators of the act be the dreadful consequences; on their heads be the dishonor, but on yours may fall the punishment. On your unhappy State will inevitably fall all the evils of the conflict you force upon the government of your country.[97]

As Thomas Hart Benton read it, the proclamation was skillfully designed to make "the mass of the people think the Union is attacked, and that the Proclamation is to save it, and that brief view is decisive with them." [98]

South Carolina responded quickly to Jackson's appeal. Governor Hayne issued his own proclamation, urging the citizens of his state to pay no attention to the President, and to prepare to defend their liberties. On December 20, he named military aides and began issuing instructions for mobilizing state troops. At the same time, Jackson fortified federal installations in the port of Charleston, and sent General Winfield Scott there to direct military activities in the dispute. But in spite of the saber-rattling, both sides acted cautiously. Jackson specifically warned Scott not to take any provocative steps, and Hayne was equally restrained. Indeed, the only faction pushing for action was the Unionists who, angered by the test oath, urged Jackson to move against the Nullifiers and even mobilized their own militia companies, armed with weapons from federal arsenals.

As the controversy simmered, Congress convened, and the administration pressed its plans for tariff reform. The vehicle was a bill sponsored by Gulian Verplanck, chairman of the House Ways and Means Committee, which called for immediate and sweeping reductions of about 50 percent in tariff schedules. But the Verplanck bill was unacceptable to the South because it retained the principle of protection and because it did not reduce duties far enough to meet South Carolina's demands. At the same time, Jackson stiffened Southern resistance by introducing the Force Bill, which specified the President's authority to take military action if he saw fit. The Judiciary Committee reported out the bill on January 21 and, on that same day, South Carolina took a step back from confrontation by delaying its enforcement of the ordinance, which was to go into effect on February 1.

During the bitter debate in the Senate over the Force Bill, Henry Clay realized that some tariff revision was inevitable, and set to work on a compromise. After consultation with Calhoun, Clay introduced his own bill based on the principle Hayne had enunciated in the 1832 debate on the tariff. His proposal provided for gradual reductions every two years of all tariffs over 20 percent until 1840, when two sharp reductions would bring all duties below the top limit of 20 percent. In doing so, the principle of protection was finally abandoned, although the fact of protection was continued for nearly a decade to permit manufacturers to accommodate to the new system. Calhoun immediately spoke in favor of the bill, and it became clear that a basis for settlement was at hand.

When the Force Bill came to a vote on February 20, most Southern senators walked out, leaving only John Tyler of Virginia to cast his vote against it. (Clay had left the floor a bit earlier, complaining of "bad air.") [99] The bill passed 32 to 1, in spite of Calhoun's fervent argument that the Congress was creating "a government of the sword." [100] On February 26, the compromise tariff passed the House, 119 to 85. The bill had strong support from the South and the West, and was opposed by New England and the Middle Atlantic states.

On March 2, Jackson signed both the compromise tariff, which was designed to save face for the South, and the Force Bill, which was designed to save face for the President.

Immediately after passage of the tariff, Calhoun hurried home in a mail cart, making the trip in half the time it usually took in a stage-coach. He arrived just as the nullification convention was reconvening to consider its response to the tariff compromise. Some members, like Dr. Thomas Cooper, were dissatisfied because it provided less than the convention had originally asked. But Calhoun and his supporters had their way. On March 15—Andrew Jackson's sixty-fifth birthday—the convention repealed the nullification ordinance by a vote of 153 to 4. It also passed an ordinance nullifying the Force Bill, but the danger was passed and the conflict ended.

In short-range terms, South Carolina won the struggle. At their insistence, the tariff was modified and the national government was forced to yield to their demands. The skirmish, which in so many ways (even down to the military maneuvering in the the harbor at Charleston) rehearsed the open conflict over slavery which followed, ended without secession, and the South fought its battle within the confines of the Union for nearly thirty more years. But Jackson won, too. In his terms, the greatest success was keeping South Carolina in the Union; yet in that effort he had help from many Southerners, some of them Nullifiers. Equally important in the long run, Jackson successfully smashed nullification and state interposition as a peaceful remedy, so that when the political battle over slavery began two decades later, that moderate middleground no longer existed. Room for maneuver was substantially decreased, and the distance between limited regime conflict and full-scale authority crisis was substantially foreshortened.

5 / PATTERNS OF POLITICS

I BEGAN this essay by arguing against one conventional view of American politics, which portrays the United States as free from significant conflict over essential characteristics of its political regime. If taxes and other extractive policies qualify as central features of the regime, then the disputes over the creation and expansion of America's financial policies described in the preceding pages provide some excellent examples of regime conflict, and show that in many instances extension of the power of the central government in the United States provoked the same kind of political conflict that accompanied similar state-building activities in Western Europe. Thus, politics in America was not always characterized by consensus, important though its liberal cultural background may be, and American politics cannot be fit into a single consensual pattern. In many cases, as national political leaders tried to increase the capacity or change the impact of the extractive system, they met with threats of noncompliance and resistance to such transformations of the regime. Federal officials responded with coercive action to enforce their policies or offered concessions to powerful challenging groups.

But this argument is still too simple. These cases will not support the generalization that all instances of tax politics, because they concern a central feature of the regime, will fit the broad pattern outlined above. Indeed, it is quite obvious that some alterations of the tax system did not provoke this kind of regime conflict. Between 1789 and 1816, tariff schedules increased frequently without popular resistance or major dispute within the elite. Moreover, in 1813, the Jeffersonians reinstated an internal tax system which had been a source of bitter contention under Federalist rule, and tax payments were made quickly and without hint of noncompliance. In brief, even cases limited to transformation of a single regime variable cannot be subsumed into one invariant pattern of political behavior.

Such is the experience of most students of American politics. Because of its long history, its institutional diversity, and its vast scale, the United States is marked by a complex and sometimes bewildering mosaic of political activity. That remarkable heterogeneity has animated a persistent search to discover and understand patterns in American politics. One of the first successful examples was V. O. Key's effort to construct a taxonomy of elections.[1] In recent years, however, the most influential attempt at classification has been the policy taxonomy developed by Theodore J. Lowi. In his original formulation, Lowi identified three types of politics—distributive, regulatory, and redistributive—and suggested that each was distinguished by its own "characteristic political structure, political process, elites, and group relations," which constituted three different "arenas of power."[2]

The criterion for classifying political events or the cases that describe them into these three categories was the nature of the output of the policy at issue or, more specifically, the extent to which that output could be disaggregated. If, like legislation on rivers and harbors, the policy output could be almost infinitely disaggregated and "dispensed by unit by small unit, each unit more or less in isolation from other units and from any general rule,"[3] then the policy was distributive. The pattern of politics associated with that arena most resembled that described by E. E. Schattschneider in *Politics, Pressures, and the Tariff,*[4] with the congressional committee (or occasionally an administrative agency) providing the locus of decision, and with logrolling the characteristic pattern of mutual association. If, like legislation controlling pricing or advertising in interstate commerce, the output of the policy was disaggregable only to the level of a "sector" (which was the rough equivalent of an industry), then the policy was regulatory. The pattern of politics resembled that described by the pluralists; the decisional locus was on the floor of Congress, and the characteristic associational pattern was the classic coalition, whose members must bargain and compromise with one another. Finally, if the output of the policy was disaggregable only at the level of large, classlike social units, then the arena was redistributive, and the characteristic political pattern was elitist. Decisions were made in the executive branch and in the upper levels of peak associations, and conflict in the arena often took on an ideological tone.

In later work, Lowi added a fourth category which he called constituent policies, pointing out, for example, that the distinctive role of American political parties could best be found in *"constituent or constitutional* processes. They all had something to do with the structure or composition of regimes, the recruitment of leaders, the size and composition of electorates, the structures of decision-making." [5] Elsewhere he simply identified constituent policies as those involving system maintenance, and said no more about them. [6]

The Lowi taxonomy represents a long step forward in the classification of political events. However, its difficulties are manifold, as Greenberg and his colleagues point out. [7] Even in later reworkings, [8] Lowi's criteria for classification are opaque in their definition and ambiguous in their application. More serious is the problem I found when I tried to fit my case materials on taxes into Lowi's categories. In his model, political events are distinguishable on the basis of inherent properties discernible in the policies themselves. Political actors look at a policy proposal and determine to what extent that policy's output can be disaggregated. (In his later formulation, political actors determine how immediate the coercive impact of a policy is, and how that coercion is to be applied.) On the basis of that assessment, they decide how to act. Thus a logical chain connects the properties of the policy with the patterns of political behavior that accompany it.

But an insoluble dilemma arises when cases describing two policy issues altogether alike in their inherent properties nevertheless exhibit altogether different patterns of politics. For example, neither the nature of the outputs nor the coercive apparatus of tariff increases of a given size changed over the years. But tariff changes were a subject of great national controversy between 1781 and 1787 and again from the Jacksonian period to the Civil War, while substantially similar revisions were made quietly and without public outcry in the years between 1789 and 1816. The Lowi schema—which "begins with the assumption that *policies determine politics*" [9]—simply cannot account for instances where apparently identical policies yield evidence of very different politics. The typology introduced below can handle that problem.

AN ALTERNATIVE TYPOLOGY

From one perspective, this essay might be described as an inquiry into the "politics of taxation." However, the present concern is not with similarities among cases of tax politics, but rather with the identification and categorization of significant variations in political behavior within that issue-area. At the same time, because of its concentration on pattern and its concern with taxonomy, the approach adopted in this chapter both resembles and seeks to comment critically upon Lowi's work on "arenas of power." (Indeed, the two typologies do show some relationship, as Figure 5.2 indicates.) But the crucial variables discussed here are not inherent in the policy itself, but involve instead situational factors; I assume, first, that relevant political actors take into account the effect of policies on established regime limits; and second, that their behavior is patterned in important ways by their perceptions of crisis. By introducing these variables, I hope to show that American politics can be subdivided into *normal politics, regime politics,* and two kinds of *crisis politics.* I believe that the use of this scheme of analysis provides a number of new insights into patterns and relationships in American politics. I have discussed the concept of a regime at some length. But "crisis" is a term which political science often employs, but rarely discusses. I will try to make clear the ways in which I think the concept can be most fruitfully used.

CRISIS

Students of politics have frequently asserted that crisis has an effect in patterning political behavior—some scholars, for example, have pointed to the importance of wars and economic crises in the emergence of a powerful presidency.[10] But social scientists have never been very precise in their definitions of crisis. James A. Robinson has pointed out that the word has been used in two quite different meanings. First, it is sometimes used to denote situations where high stress, panic, disaster, or violence are observable. Second, it is also used to indicate a turning point when the status of a system changes from a satisfactory to a dangerous condition, a meaning originally derived from medical terminology.[11] In this essay, the term will more closely resemble Robinson's second usage. But even more helpful is a definition offered by a Missouri hospital as it cared for Harry S. Truman during the last few weeks of his life. When that institution placed Truman on its critical list, reporters pressed for a definition of the term "critical." A hospital spokesman replied: "Vital signs are unstable and not within normal limits. There are major complications. Death may be imminent." [12] While it may not be possible to determine when a socioeconomic or political system is near death, I believe that crucial variables, analogous to vital signs in humans, can be established for them, and that a crisis is at hand when members of a system perceive that the normal limits of one or more of those variables have been or soon may be breached.

Two kinds of crises can be distinguished. During wars, depressions, natural disasters, or other kinds of *environmental crises,** all the relevant political actors—elite and mass publics alike—generally agree that "vital signs" describing the health of the society as a whole are or soon will be outside of normal limits. In most political systems, the state apparatus is expected to act to meet such exogenous threats, and politics under conditions of this kind can be very different from politics in more settled times. Of course, the distinction between crisis and constitutional government is not a new one, and many political systems have had established contingency systems for governance during crisis situations. The constitutional structure of the Roman Republic provided for a temporary dictator to guide the state in emergencies and the contemporary constitutions of the Fifth French Republic and the state of India provide remarkably far-reaching powers for chief executives during crises.[13] Nor is it necessary for such powers to be formally established in a written constitution. In his work in progress on the American presidency, James S. Young suggests that the regime that governs this nation has come to include a fairly regularized contingency system of government, with the presidency assuming special powers and responsibilities during periods of crises. In other nations, there are frequent examples in this and other centuries of chief executives declaring extraconstitutional protectivist dictatorships during real or apparent emergencies.[14]

---

* Admittedly, this term is a bit confusing in this time of concern over the earth's natural environment. But the term already has some currency in the jargon of political science, and it seems useless to proliferate new terms when old ones will serve. See Almond, Flanagan, and Mundt, eds., *Crisis, Choice, and Change* p. 48.

If those contingency systems fail to resolve a crisis, or if the political elite is incapable of "managing" challenge to the regime, a different kind of crisis can result. The vital signs which are unstable concern mass compliance with the political order, not the society as a whole. What is in jeopardy is not simply social stability, but elite control,[15] and what the French call a *crise de regime* is at hand. In the post-colonial history of America, the only situation which unequivocally meets this criterion is the Civil War, where withdrawal of support by an entire region and conflict over the goals and activities of the state precipitated what is called here an *authority crisis*.

If the distinction between environmental and authority crises seems difficult to grasp, consider for a moment a baseball team. If the squad suddenly lost forty games in a row, or if none of its players were batting over .180, or if all its pitchers had sore arms at the same time, that team would be experiencing an environmental crisis of some magnitude. Presumably, all the players and staff of the team would agree that such a crisis was at hand, and the odds are good that the general manager or the team owners would undertake extraordinary steps, making frantic trades or hiring a new manager. When the crisis had abated, normal operating procedures would be reestablished. But if the players on a team refused to bring bats to the plate, or if the outfielders went out to their positions and took off their shirts so they could sunbathe, or if the hitters decided to run the wrong way around the bases in spite of admonishments from their managers and the umpires, a different sort of crisis would be at hand, and that team would, in fact, no longer be playing baseball. In that situation, which corresponds to an authority crisis in politics, it is more difficult to predict what action the general manager or owner might take.

Among political scientists, "crisis" is sometimes used in still another sense to denote situations where an academic observer has identified the threat of change, regardless of the perceptions of the political actors involved. Thus, as Raymond Grew and his colleagues struggled to define "crisis," they began by proposing that it might mean "any serious threat to the functioning of a political regime," a definition quite congruent with either notion of crisis as used here. But they soon found this interpretation too limiting: "The threats to system and even fundamental changes are often masked by custom or imperception as well as political skill. Historical figures saw threats historians now discount and overlooked some that later proved serious. If the emphasis on self-awareness in the process of political changes seems valuable, the fact remains that the historian cannot be dependent on the judgment of dead politicians."

So Grew and his colleagues added a second definitional criterion: crisis was also indicated by "*an important change in the way politics worked—*by new institutions or changes in the political process." [16] And Flanagan and Mundt began their work with a definition of a political crisis as that time when "alternative courses of development become salient issues, and tensions rise to the point where significant structural changes become possible." [17]

Two problems with these definitions are immediately apparent. First, it is an empirical fact that, at least in the American political system, large-scale regime alteration can take place without "serious threat to the functioning of a political regime." Changes of substantial magnitude are often "managed" by the political elite with little danger of full-scale breakdown, so it is difficult to equate "an important change in the way politics works" with "crisis." Indeed, in the United States, regime change without crisis seems the rule rather than the exception, and I believe that the distinction just made between *regime politics* and *authority crisis* is therefore essential for any adequate analysis and description of political change in America.

Second, and equally important, this essay attempts to examine the way situational variables like crisis and regime boundaries affect the behavior of real-life political actors. But without the stipulation that the participants themselves must perceive crises, there is no way to explain why those actors change their behavior in such situations. The causal link between perceptions and observable changes of behavior simply vanishes. So here I will restrict my usage of "crisis" to situations where the relevant political actors themselves believe that the society as a whole is threatened by environmental crisis, or to situations where the political elite or its opponents recognize that an authority crisis has undermined elite control. "Crises" which are only perceived after the fact by political scientists will be ignored.

INTRODUCING THE TAXONOMY

Like the Lowi scheme in its expanded form, my typology is based on a pair of dichotomous variables. (See Figure 5.1 for a diagramatic presentation.) An initial assumption is that when faced with a policy initiative, political actors will assess the impact of that policy on the settled outlines of

Figure 5.1 A Typology of Political Events

Is the status of the system
perceived to be critical?

	Authority crisis	Environmental crisis
Yes	Authority crisis	Environmental crisis
No	Regime politics	Normal politics

Yes	No

Are regime boundaries perceived
to be at issue?

the political regime. On the one hand, those actors may conclude that a policy proposal is contained within and implies no substantial change in regime boundaries. Alternatively, they may feel that implementation of a policy initiative would involve some fundamental change in the settled limits of the regime.

In the first case, where no relevant actors perceive substantial change in regime boundaries, a policy issue will be considered an instance of *normal politics* and, I suggest, the pattern of political behavior will exhibit high conformity to established norms of day-to-day political conduct. In America, that means that conflict will be of limited intensity and duration; such conflict will be contained within existing institutional structures and, when implemented, the policies will meet with compliance from affected publics at a reasonably high level.

In the second case, where actors perceive some redefinition of the regime, the policy at issue will be considered an instance of *regime politics,* and political behavior will display a different pattern, since some portion of the fundamental rules and settlements of politics are themselves at issue. Conflict will be more intense; normally dormant groups (which may include economic classes or major geographical regions) often join in the struggle; conflict may extend beyond its normal institutional limits; and compliance with policies as implemented may be highly problematic.

This distinction between issues which are contained within regime boundaries and issues which imply changes of those boundaries is diagramed on the horizontal dimension of Figure 5.1. Although David Easton does not use the same terms, a similar distinction between regime and normal politics (he calls the latter "allocative politics") is important in his work.[18] Unfortunately, that distinction is generally ignored by his readers, who take his generalizations about systems inputs and outputs, which are of some use in the context of regime politics, and try to apply them to the study of normal politics, where they make very little sense.

But the distinction between normal and regime politics, helpful though it may sometimes be in understanding the pattern of politics associated with different kinds of issues, is inadequate in and of itself. Instances arise where the actions of political leaders clearly exceed established regime boundaries, but where the other actors seem uncharacteristically docile and compliant, as the case of the 1813 internal revenue system demonstrates. To deal with this dilemma, it is helpful to assume that at the same time political participants are pondering the impact of a policy proposal on the established regime structure, they are also monitoring the overall status of the political, socioeconomic, and international systems, and when they agree that those systems are in crisis, they alter their behavior (see the vertical dimension of Figure 5.1).

In an *environmental crisis*, such as war, depression, famine, or even severe shortages of key resources, citizens may put aside their objections to extraordinary political initiatives, and one or more actors may be authorized to act outside the normal limits of the regime, so long as those actions are temporary and clearly related to the emergency at hand. (It should also be noted that the definition of the broad categories of crisis variables can in itself be an important regime issue. For example, the central government in the United States has not always had clear responsibility for the maintenance of the national economy, in part because no adequate tools for dealing with economic crisis existed. So whether or not a depression is a crisis which authorizes political action is a question that cannot be answered without examining the regime structure at any given time.)

As suggested earlier, some crises are not the result of environmental factors, but instead stem from a failure of or a large-scale attack upon the political order itself. Unfortunately, none of the examples of tax politics examined here provide much insight into such *authority crises*, although the nullification movement that grew out of struggles over the tariff nearly provoked such a crisis. For that reason, my conclusions about political behavior in such periods must be speculative. On the one hand, since the whole structure of rules governing political conduct is called into question in such situations, it seems unreasonable to expect that structured patterns of behavior will exist for the management of authority crises like those that have evolved to deal with environmental crises. On the other hand, some systems which have experienced chronic authority crises have

developed distinctive strategies for coping with them. The French seem
to follow intricate rituals during *crises de regime*,[19] and the military has a
well-defined and predictable role during authority crises in many Latin
American countries.

I should emphasize that just as the distinction between regime and normal politics has its root in the perceptions of political actors, so the definition of crisis must involve the perceptions of the political elite and the
mass of citizens. Those perceptions may be imprecise, and different sets
of participants may in fact reach different conclusions about the potential
effects of a policy proposal or the status of the socioeconomic and political
systems. For instance, the dispute over the seizure of the steel mills in
1952 seems in large part a disagreement about Truman's definition of the
situation as a crisis, a definition which was successfully disputed by
members of the governing elite. Often, then, supporters or opponents of a
policy may deny or disguise the regime effects of their proposal, or may
work to convince other actors that crises are real or feigned. The previous
materials on tax politics provided some indications of the ways in which
participants arrive at these perceptions of crisis or regime effects, and how
those perceptions modify their normal patterns of political behavior.

Finally, it is worthwhile to examine very briefly the way in which the
categories in this taxonomy related to those proposed by Lowi. As Harry
Eckstein points out, the most widely used classificatory strategy is a
method which might be called "progressive differentiation." With a
broad and heterogeneous subject matter like "organisms" (or "politics"),
an analyst divides that subject matter in a number of categories, like the
plant and animal kingdoms, so that variance within those categories is
reduced. Successive classificatory cuts are constructed (dividing organisms
further into phyla, classes, and orders, for instance) until some compelling
end point is found.[20] In Figure 5.2 I suggest that the taxonomy offered
here might be a useful first approximation, and Lowi's categories can be
generally understood as a subcategory of normal politics. But that is a bit
too simple. Lowi's "constituent" category is probably congruent with
regime politics, and some of his instances of redistribution fit in that category as well. But other redistributive policies and all regulatory and distributive cases fit well into the class of normal politics, and I believe that
the Lowi typology therefore provides a valuable starting point for systematic analysis of that important category.

Figure 5.2 "Progressive Differentiation" and the Taxonomy of Political Events

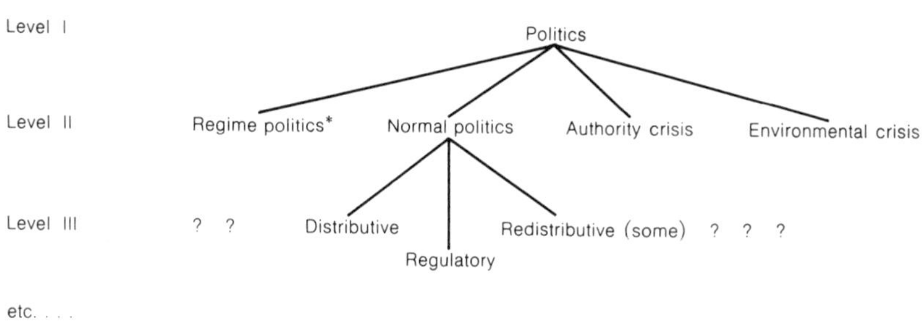

*Includes "constituent" and some "redistributive" issues.

CLASSIFYING TAX POLITICS

Although several of the tax disputes described in previous chapters represent mixed cases, they can be usefully analyzed as examples of regime, normal, and crisis politics, as suggested by my taxonomy. Tariff politics between 1789 (when the first tariff was passed) and 1816 (when protection became the main point of contention) seem to fit neatly into the category of normal politics. The struggles over the initial extractive framework and over the whiskey excise are relatively pure cases of regime politics, while the passage of internal taxes in 1813 illustrates the dynamics of politics during environmental crises. Tariff politics after 1816 is harder to classify, but the disputes obviously involved regime questions; in fact, the movement for nullification almost precipitated an authority crisis. Finally, the fight over the direct tax of 1798 had elements of regime conflict, but because of the threat of war with France, most participants defined the situation as an environmental crisis. Figure 5.3 attempts to locate the cases of tax politics schematically in the policy space of the taxonomy. Although the number of cases is obviously small and authority crisis is, for all intents and purposes, an empty box, some tentative comments about patterns of politics in each category seem in order.

NORMAL POLITICS

The day-to-day activities of normal politics are not often dramatic. Conflict occurs, but because regime parameters define and limit both the pos-

Figure 5.3 Classification of Tax Politics, 1781-1833

REGIME POLITICS	AUTHORITY CRISIS
Building the extractive framework	
Whiskey excise, 1791	
Tariff, 1824-1833	
NORMAL POLITICS	ENVIRONMENTAL CRISIS
Tariff, 1789-1816	Internal taxes, 1813-1816

sible solutions to those disputes and the number of authorized participants, that conflict is muted and its resolution relatively routine. Broad
outlines of preexisting policy contain normal conflict, and participants are
those who have already won favored statuses in earlier regime battles. As
indications of that favored status, participants in normal politics are
granted some degree of veto power over decision-making in the policy
areas that touch their interests. Thus, in early tariff decisions after 1789,
the expressed desires of any given state's congressional delegation were
given weight in determining the objects and levels of tariff duties for
products manfactured or grown in their states.

The benefits distributed in normal politics are concrete. Thus, manufacturers and merchants were favored with tariff protection, bounties, and
the like. But the costs to participants are primarily symbolic, a pattern
Murray Edelman sees continuing into modern politics.[21] In the first years
of the Republic, some manufacturers (the snuff and loaf sugar industries,
for example) paid small excises which they were able to pass on to consumers. Southern aristocrats were also forced to bear minor taxes on their
most ostentatious luxuries, such as their carriages. Like the regulation of
corporations in this century, those symbolic penalties seemed designed to
prove to the mass of citizens that favored participants were not getting
away altogether free—even when they were. The whiskey distillers raised
no serious protest when they believed that the excise was symbolic in nature, and would not be enforced. When they realized, however, that they
were being asked to bear substantial concrete costs, the dispute escalated
into regime conflict.

The arena in which normal conflict takes place is generally well-established. In early tariff politics, policy disputes were usually resolved on the floor of the House of Representatives, and the recommendations of the House Ways and Means Committee seemed especially important after 1794, when Gallatin arrived in Washington. In contrast, later regime disputes over tariffs spilled over into the Senate, into state legislatures, and even into the streets. In contemporary American politics, the arena of normal politics is even more clearly defined, with most such disputes and allocations taking place within well-bounded subsystems consisting of one or more congressional committees, a bureau in the executive branch, and one or more interest groups.[22]

The strategy of conflict in normal politics also seems regular and well-defined. Since rewards but not costs are being allocated, logrolling coalitions have been a feature of normal politics since its inception. On tariff questions, congressmen deferred to representatives of other states on policy questions that did not touch upon their own interests, and every state could get protection for its special crops or products. Moreover, when disputes arose, routine bargaining and negotiation were sufficient to resolve them. Indeed, the earliest sign that tariff questions were shifting from normal to regime politics was the breakdown in logrolling that took place after 1816.

Finally, because decisions that result from normal politics are by definition contained within preexisting regime boundaries, management of compliance is not a difficult task for the political elite. Thus, when the tariff passed from a regime to a normal issue after 1789, smuggling declined quickly, and shippers themselves banded together to urge compliance with tariff laws. Since citizens are not aroused to resistance by the allocations of normal politics, routine administration is usually sufficient to implement those decisions, and Alexander Hamilton's new bureaucracy was more than adequate to the task.

Thus, normal politics is characterized by muted conflict, by a limited number of established participants, by a well-defined institutional arena for decision-making, patterns of logrolling, negotiation, and compromise, and by implementation of decisions through routine administration. In those broad characteristics, normal politics in the first half-century of American politics seems very much like normal politics in the twentieth century, as described by contemporary pluralist scholars.

REGIME POLITICS

If conflict in normal politics is muted and contained, conflict in regime politics is highly visible, dramatic, and difficult to circumscribe. Regime conflict involves the most fundamental kind of political questions; the farmers on the frontier in Pennsylvania believed that the whiskey excise was a heavy and unwarranted tax on an essential commodity and item of exchange, and the planters in the South feared that the tariff would choke off their vital export trade. Participants are, therefore, strongly moved by such disputes, and may threaten noncompliance with the policies in question.

When faced with a regime issue, people are likely to attempt some accounting, however gross and unscientific, of their status under changing regime boundaries, and they will inevitably compare their future status with their position under the existing regime. The whiskey excise forced upon the frontier the realization that Eastern interests were the major beneficiaries of the activities of the new government. In much the same way, the dispute over the tariff made it clear to the South that their supposed position of equality in the new regime was endangered, and that without some mechanism to guarantee veto rights over majority decisions the entire slave system could be jeopardized. Because dispute over a single feature of a regime can cause people to reevaluate their whole relationship to that regime (and "calculate the value of the Union" anew), it is easy to understand how regime politics can escalate to full-scale authority crises, unless "managed" and resolved by an adept elite.

Moreover, conflicts over regimes mobilize participants who are not usually involved in the day-to-day bargaining of normal politics. Otherwise dormant regional groupings (like the South in the dispute over protective tariffs); classlike economic groups (like debtors in the debate over funding and assumption or creditors during the fight for an impost in 1781); and other occasional participants (like frontier farmers or the Continental Army) are caught up by regime issues, in a process that very much resembles the mobilization of potential groups as described by David Truman. That element of Truman's schema has always seemed out of place in *The Governmental Process* which deals with normal, everyday politics,[23] but it makes good sense in the context of regime politics.

Regime issues expand the arenas for political conflict. In the cases studied here, debate in Congress was merely the first stage for conflict. Both the fight over the impost in the 1780s and the battles over protective tariffs spread quickly to state legislatures and influenced state elections. Moreover, conflict over the regime sometimes bring into play new, ad hoc institutions and procedures. When defeated in the states, proponents of the impost of 1781 called together a constitutional convention to revise the Articles of Confederation. The whiskey rebels created their own steering committee (and considered reconstituting their six counties as a separate political entity). The tariff disputes saw the creation of a "peak" lobbying organization at the Harrisburg convention; and the nullifiers proposed a whole new set of constitutional procedures, designed to assure them veto rights over new regime alterations. Regime politics can even spill out into the streets, with violence an occasional weapon, as illustrated by the whiskey rebels, the battles in South Carolina during the elections of 1830, and the threat of violence from the Continental Army in 1783.

Because regime issues involve the allocation of concrete costs as well as benefits, participants tend to view them in zero-sum terms. The whiskey rebels believed that their tax payments made it possible for Easterners to avoid heavier land taxes, and Southern planters felt that the tariff took money from their pockets and put it into the tills of Northern manufacturers. In normal politics, it is possible that all participants will believe they benefit from a new policy. In regime conflicts (and especially in tax disputes), the dollars paid out by one group are perceived to be benefits to others. Thus, the patterns useful for the resolution of normal disputes are no longer applicable. Logrolling cannot settle an argument if participants see the conflict in zero-sum terms. However, relatively standard tactics for the resolution of regime conflict sometimes do exist and those techniques change over time. In the period under discussion here, the "grand compromise" was the dominant tactic for settling large-scale disputes over the regime. The debate over funding and assumption was resolved when support for Hamilton's fiscal package was traded for relocation of the national capital and revision of procedures for settling state accounts with the national government. Forty years later, another "grand compromise" bargained away protection over a period of years in return for withdrawal of the threat of nullification.

Finally, since changes in regime limits represent changes in firmly established patterns of political behavior, and since those disputes are frequently bitter ones, compliance in such situations is generally highly problematic. No habits of obedience to new commands exist; some participants in the zero-sum conflict believe they are losers; and routine administration will usually prove inadequate for maintaining compliance. Costs of enforcing new orders may be high, as they were in the cases of the whiskey excise and the direct tax of 1798, and heavy doses of both coercion and legitimating symbols may be required to establish new patterns of behavior. Cases of regime politics are, therefore, likely to yield the richest data for the study of elite techniques and strategies for exacting compliance and maintaining social control.

Lowi has made a useful start in defining subcategories of normal politics; in much the same way, more data on regime conflict should make it possible to distinguish between subtypes of regime politics. Some of the cases here describe the creation of state authority where none existed before, and it was clear that Hamilton and Washington were concerned about the fragile nature of the new federal government's authority when they sent troops off to quell the whiskey rebellion. But that kind of "primitive accumulation" of political capital may turn out to look very different from the political patterns which arise in disputes over altering or expanding the authority of already existing regimes.

ENVIRONMENTAL CRISIS

Patterns of politics during environmental crises are very different from politics during normal and regime conflict. While political actors may disagree about the substance of policy, that disagreement is not converted into political conflict, and elite domination of policy-making is not challenged. Indeed, if the elite can successfully establish its definition of a situation as a crisis, it can undertake without direct opposition activities which might otherwise be considered gross violations of regime boundaries. In 1798, the government levied an unpopular direct tax, and that tax included a radical schedule of progressive duties on houses, but because those taxes were justified by the threat of war with France, little opposition arose. In 1813, the Congress reimposed an entire system of internal taxes that had been mightily disputed two decades earlier, and because those taxes were temporary and provided revenues for the war against Britain, they were paid promptly and without complaint.

Since conflict over policy tends to disappear in crises, there is little basis for the analysis of strategies contestants may have used or patterns of conflict resolution most likely to be followed. Nor is maintenance of compliance problematic. Indeed, it is the extraordinarily high level of unquestioning obedience to unprecedented commands that is the most striking feature of crisis politics. Herbert Simon says that an authority relationship exists when a subordinate "holds in abeyance his own critical faculties for choosing between alternatives and uses the formal criterion of the receipt of a command or signal as his basis for choice." [24] Elite authority is most readily apparent in crisis situations, when all relevant actors seem to temporarily suspend their own evaluations of policies and act as directed by the crisis managers.

However, if political conflict is not evident during a crisis, it is often visible during the initial definition of a situation as critical. No new taxes were levied until after war was officially declared in 1812; and the lack of any clear and formal definition of an emergency in 1798 hindered efforts to raise funds and recruit an army. Moreover, compliance will not be automatic if commands are not obviously related to the crisis at hand, and are not limited to the duration of the emergency. Thus, collection of internal duties during the Adams administration was more difficult because of ambiguity about the relationship of those taxes to the French threat, and because of the desire of some officials to maintain those taxes in effect indefinitely. On the other hand, the taxes of 1813 were specifically labeled "war taxes," and were supposed to expire automatically when the war ended. If crisis politics is elitist, the elite cannot expect its commands to be fully authoritative unless it takes care to define a crisis unambiguously and to relate its actions to the situation at hand.

At present, it seems apparent that responsibility for crisis management is lodged in the presidency, and that presidents are expected and authorized to take extraordinary action during wars, depressions, or severe resource shortages like the "energy crisis." During the early nineteenth century, no such settled responsibility for action during crisis was evident, and the development of a well-defined "contingency system" in the presidency may well be a twentieth-century phenomenon. [25]

AUTHORITY CRISIS

Although none of the cases of tax politics studied here can be unequivocably described as an authority crisis, the nullification controversy approached that category. Some participants in the tariff struggle escalated their complaints about protection into a critique of the entire regime structure and proposed secession. In fact, if more than one state had supported nullification, an authority crisis might have developed. But the resources of the actors in opposition were too limited and their popular base too narrow to constitute a significant challenge to the entire regime. Indeed, there are very few examples of such crisis anywhere in American politics, and none that center on tax issues. The struggle against the mother country after 1765 qualifies as an authority crisis—but for the British regime. The repudiation and transformation of the infant regime between 1787 and 1789 might fit this category, had it not been managed so carefully and skillfully by the nationalist political leaders. The Civil War is an obvious case. Since that time, challenges to the regime have not seriously threatened the full structure of the nation's political norms and procedures.

Nonetheless, it is possible to make some very preliminary suggestions about the characteristics of authority crises. The participants will be the same large-scale social groupings (such as social classes and geographical regions) that mobilized for more limited contests over the regime, and conflict—which ranges over a number of regime questions—will be bitter and dramatic. Nor can that conflict be contained within existing institutions, since it is the legitimacy of those very institutions that is under challenge. The tactics for the resolution of simple regime issues (like "grand compromises") will not serve to settle authority crises, since those tactics are themselves elements of the regime and will be repudiated by some or all of the political actors. Thus, attempts in the 1850s to bring to bear the "grand compromise" technique to settle the dispute over slavery were notably unsuccessful. Indeed, it is the failure of those procedures that is the most common signal that an authority crisis is at hand. However, political systems that face repeated authority crises, like those in France or Latin America, may develop relatively standard techniques for resolution of such situations. The military coup and temporary rule by junta seems the most common pattern in developing nations.

Authority crises can have two sources. First, the political elite may prove unable to cope with an environmental crisis. A depression may continue too long, or a war may be lost, and that failure can call into question the legitimacy of the whole political order. Second, standard tactics for the resolution of conflict over the regime may fail, and the elite may be unable to "manage" disputes over some element of regime norms. As suggested earlier, challenge to the regime can then escalate, raising more and more questions about the conduct of politics. If such a challenge is supported by a significant sector of the population, an authority crisis is at hand. In either case, well-institutionalized regimes do not usually reach such an advanced stage of political disarray without poor performance within the governing elite in the face of some extraordinary test.

6 / POLITICAL CHANGE IN THE UNITED STATES

AT THE BEGINNING of this essay, I suggested that disputes over taxation might be representative of a special type of politics, and that case studies of the transformation of tax systems might therefore provide insights into patterns of conflict over the shape of America's political regime. As the taxonomy in chapter 5 makes clear, my hopeful proposition about tax politics was only partially correct; the extractive system is certainly a crucial component of the regime, but conflicts over its provisions are sometimes contained within the boundaries of normal politics, and sometimes muted by the pragmatic requirements of environmental crises.

I believe my typology provides concepts which help understand the conditions under which substantially similar policy initiatives can result in significantly different political outcomes. But my taxonomy shares with Lowi's policy scheme a number of difficulties. Whatever their heuristic usefulness, these sets of concepts are very difficult to test empirically. A post hoc finding that the Whiskey Rebellion was an example of regime politics may be instructive, but it does not help to categorize contemporary policy conflicts. Indeed, several of the problems that Greenberg and his colleagues raise in regard to Lowi's policy taxonomy apply to mine as well,[1] and all of their objections highlight the difficulties involved in making such concepts operational and putting them to use in empirical research.

Some of these problems arise because both Lowi and I rely on case data to support our arguments. In my use of these cases on taxes, I assume with Eckstein that a case can be "defined technically as a phenomenon for which we report and interpret only a single measure on any pertinant variable." [2] Nonetheless, the simple issue of when a "case" begins and when it ends can be a difficult problem, as Greenberg and his colleagues point out.[3] The case of the Whiskey Rebellion is contained within a relatively brief time period; my treatment of the protective tariff extends over seventeen years.

Obviously, I am not arguing that case data are useless. Indeed, for both Lowi's and my purposes, such data are invaluable as illustrations of different patterns or "arenas" of politics. Moreover, scholars have traditionally agreed upon the value of case studies for generating concepts and hypotheses about social and political processes. In the paradigm presented in this chapter, I have sought to use these cases on taxes (and other relevant literature) to construct a set of regime components and variables. Cases can also be used for testing hypotheses, as Eckstein points out.[4] Although I do not employ any single case in that fashion, the entire treatment of the creation and elaboration of an extractive system in the United States can be examined as a single case study, and as such can lend support to some implicit hypotheses set out by Tilly and his colleagues. For example, Tilly states that an adequate extractive system is "essential to the creation of strong states," and goes on to point to evidence that in Europe there was "tenacious and widespread resistance to the expansion of state power." [5] If this argument about Western Europe is transformed into an hypothesis about the problems of state-building in other areas of the world, my data on tax politics in the United States show that in America expansion of the state's extractive system also met with resistance from some sectors.

For case studies to be truly useful in the testing of hypotheses, they must be written with a theorectical underpinning which guarantees that variables are "consistently and systematically dealt with, . . . [not] picked up and discarded as it suits the author's convenience." [6] Almond, Flanagan, and Mundt demonstrate how productively such cases can be used in their volume, *Crisis, Choice, and Change*. Each of their case studies has been informed by a common and explicit theoretical framework, and as a result the editors can compare sequences of events in different nations to arrive at interesting, if still tentative, conclusions about causal linkages.[7]

The cases on taxation in this study provide valuable illustrations of the patterns of political behavior in instances of conflict over regime issues, and they have provided as well an opportunity to propose what I hope is a useful new set of categories for the analysis of public policy. But they do not meet the difficult criteria outlined above for hypothesis testing. Indeed, if an analyst is using case studies to search for a theoretical framework, it is impractical to suggest that at the same time, those cases should be informed by an explicit theoretical base. Moreover, case studies of any kind are inherently unsuited for precise description and measurement of patterns of regime change. Cases of regime politics can be found which do not result in change in the regime. For instance, a challenging group may raise a regime issue not in response to some elite initiative, but because it has achieved a new level of political consciousness, like blacks in the 1950s, and such challenge may be turned back by the political elite with no measurable transformation of the regime. Alternatively, cases of environmental crisis or normal politics may in fact portray significant regime change. In the United States, wars lead to rapid upward shifts in expenditures and revenue collections; at the end of hostilities, those allocative activities decline, but not to their previous levels.[8] Thus, environmental crises can lead to a permanent transformation of regime activities. Indeed, even cases of normal politics show regime changes; from 1789 to 1812, the tariff was raised often in small increments, and several such increases added up to a sizable transformation in the tariff schedule as a whole.

Since this essay deals with political change as well as patterns of political behavior, some strategy must be found which does not depend entirely on case studies if progress is to be made toward the systematic examination of change and development in the United States. Case studies should not be neglected; as suggested above, I can think of no other method to analyze those instances of regime challenge which are successfully defused by elite management and result in no significant change along any regime variable. Such instances are rare, however, and the rest of this chapter outlines a research strategy which depends upon more careful specification of a full range of regime components and related variables. I also will discuss some of the problems of finding quantitative indicators for such variables, and will argue that longitudinal analysis of those indicators is the most straightforward way to test hypotheses about political change and development in the United States.

REGIME COMPONENTS

If some students of politics occasionally seem to argue that change and development do not take place in America, others might argue that politics in the United States is nothing but change. Shifting coalitions of interest groups, different patterns of voting in legislatures, new incumbents, and other elements make pictures of the process of government in America into a continuously changing political kaleidoscope. Samuel Huntington has suggested a path out of this conundrum: "The first step in analyzing political change . . . is simply, as William Mitchell put it, to identify 'the objects that are susceptible to changes.' It is to identify what are or may be the components of a political system and then to establish what, if any, relations exist in the changes among them. Such an approach focuses on *componential change.*" [9]

Drawing on my cases of tax politics and on other relevant literature, I will try in this section to specify both the major components of a regime, and the sources of external disturbance which have the heaviest impact on regime activities. The discussion is summarized in Figure 6.1,[10] a schematic presentation of the variables and relationships which are most important in the analysis of political change and development. Studies of single regime components, like this essay on extraction, are useful but quite limited. Invariably they involve the researcher in the exploration of the interactive effects of other variables; in my cases, for instance, discussion of extractive policies often leads to description of foreign policies or elite strategies for social control.

As Alexander Hamilton's efforts must prove, change in a regime can result from the purposeful efforts of members of the political elite seeking to transform the regime from within; regime change may also result from poor performance and ineptitude on the part of the elite. However, transformation of a regime frequently represents as well elite choices in response to changes in their environment. As Figure 6.1 indicates, the key sources of such disturbance are the international environment, the nation's technoeconomic base and related social structure, and a distinguishable set of mass political opinions and behaviors. The components of the regime itself are, first and most obviously, what Almond, Flanagan,

Figure 6.1 Regime Components

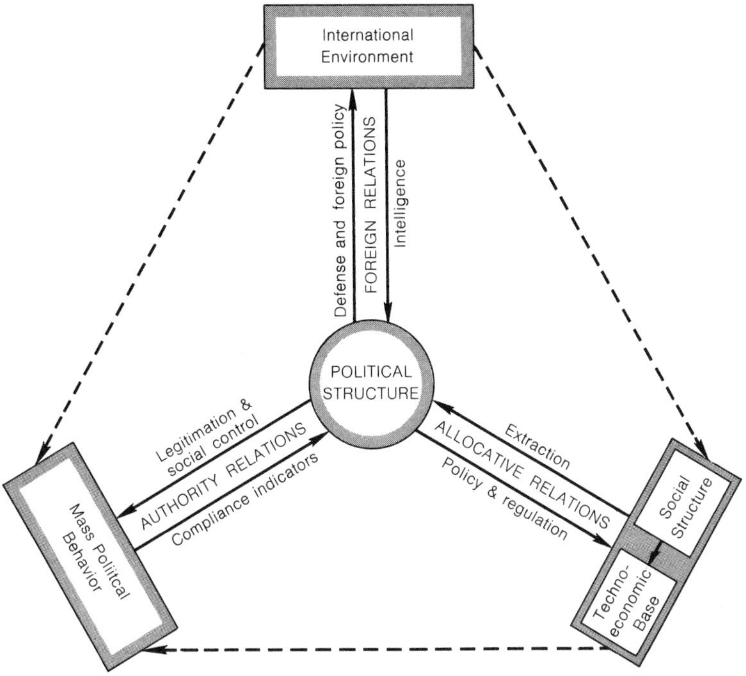

Based on Finch and Forsythe.

and Mundt call the political structure and, second, those policies and agencies that maintain and stabilize relationships between the political structure and the three sources of external stimuli specified above. To carry out the tasks of foreign relations, allocative relations, and authority relations, the political structure maintains sets of inputs from and outputs to each of those three elements, as Figure 6.1 suggests.

Although I use the terms "inputs" and "outputs," I have not uncritically adopted David Easton's systems paradigm. In the Eastonian model, "demands" and "supports" come from the "environment" into the political system, and "outputs" are produced by some conversion process within the political system and returned to the environment. But without much more careful specification of the objects of political control (which must of course include the subject population in a nation), this model fosters the impression that a flow of data about what the public thinks and wants ("inputs") produces and determines what the government does ("outputs").[11] This rather fuzzy picture has a pleasant correspondence to traditional democratic dogma: the people speak, the government acts. In this essay, however, I assume that elite actors determine their own choices, and that so long as they can convince the subject population to supply necessary inputs (especially revenues), those choices will generally prevail. Thus, I assume that elite outputs in the area of social control and legitimation are intended to control and sometimes alter attitudes of the subject population. As Murray Edelman puts it, "political actions chiefly arouse or satisfy people not by granting or withholding their stable substantive demands, but rather by changing the demands and expectations." [12] Similarly, allocative outputs from the regime are designed to control and sometimes alter the behavior of the technoeconomic base, and outputs to the international environment are intended to control the activities of other states.

In Figure 6.1, broken lines depict three other linkages which are intrinsically important, but of only secondary interest in the exposition of this study. One such connection is the intermittent and highly problematic relationship between the subject population in its class and status roles, and the development of consciousness in "citizen" and other political roles. Another is the link from the international environment to mass political opinions, a relationship that exists when another nation seeks to influence directly the subject population in a target state. Citizen Genet's propaganda efforts in the United States in 1793 and broadcasts overseas by the Voice of America today are examples of activities designed to achieve such influence. Finally, a third linkage is the direct interaction between the international environment and a nation's technoeconomic base. In this century, international depressions, price increases by suppliers of raw materials, and other economic policies by trading partners have damaged the economy of the United States. But this effect is even more important in developing nations. During the Napoleonic Wars, for instance, French and British policies toward international shipping had a serious impact on the American economy.

INTERNATIONAL ENVIRONMENT

As earlier chapters indicate, such international disturbances as the War of 1812 and the near war with France in the 1790s can lead to alteration of extractive policies and can have other important consequences for the activities of the regime. Levels of expenditures are transformed. Previously stable patterns of interaction between institutions within the political structure are altered, as the shifting relationship between Presidents and Congress demonstrates. Government controls over economic activity change markedly during wars. Failure in war may lead to protest and challenge to a regime; however, threats of war and success in military action may promote consensus and increase support for the regime, as illustrated by the case of internal revenues during the War of 1812.

Students of domestic politics in the United States often overlook the importance of stimuli from the international environment. As Gabriel Almond suggests, "the international environment has been almost completely neglected as a factor influencing stability and change, a most serious ommission indeed." [13] And Charles Tilly adds his own lament: "In my review of recent writings, I have encountered impressively little discussion of the way the structure of world markets, the operation of economic imperialism, and the characteristics of the international state system affect the pattern of political change in different parts of the world. Our review of the West European experience, on the other hand, has often brought us face to face with these very phenomena." [14] In short, no sophisticated understanding of the process of political change and development seems possible if stimuli from the international environment are ignored.

TECHNOECONOMIC BASE AND SOCIAL STRUCTURE

Since Marx, social scientists have assumed that changes in the technoeconomic base of a nation will have some impact on its politics. Nevertheless, this insight is rarely consistently applied to the study of political change and development in the United States. A few scholars have incorporated the notion of stimuli from the technoeconomic base into their conceptual models. For example, Walter Dean Burnham assumes that realigning elections are an indirect result of tranformations in the nation's socioeconomic base. As he puts it, "critical realignments . . . arise out of increasingly visible social maladjustments; these in turn are the product of transformation in a quite separately developing socioeconomic system." [15] Some social movement theorists also relate increases in the frequency of protest behavior to such stimuli. Roberta Ash, for example, writes: "Ultimately social movements are caused by transformations of the material substructure, but it is more useful to analyze them as reflections of transformations of the relations of production." [16] Her statement also highlights the importance of distinguishing between changes in the technoeconomic base as such, and transformations in the related social structure; disturbances of the latter kind often lead directly to the tensions and constituencies which create mass protest.

Economic collapse can shrink government revenues and force changes in policies. It can also energize protest groups and provide opportunities for new social control strategies. Piven and Cloward have described the impact of economic dislocation in this fashion: "Mass unemployment that persists for any length of time diminishes the capacity of other institutions to bind and constrain people. . . . When large numbers of people are suddenly barred from their traditional occupations, the entire structure of social control is weakened and may even collapse. . . . [I]f the dislocation is widespread, the legitimacy of the social order itself may come to be questioned." [17]

Demographic change can also alter political behavior. During the tariff battles, uneven population growth in different regions shifted the balance of political power in Congress, and contemporary studies of voting behavior have shown the impact of both resettlement patterns and generational change on party support.[18] Finally, the class and status roles that are built upon a nation's socioeconomic base are a central factor in organizing or inhibiting the development of political consciousness and mass political action.

MASS POLITICAL BEHAVIOR

Changing voting patterns, levels of protest activity, and opinions about political efficacy and the legitimacy of government are all factors of importance in the analysis of regime change. Marxist analysts look for an eventual convergence between these political opinions and the attitudes of the subject population in its class roles; they assume that eventually all of the members of subordinate economic classes will become alienated from the political system. In liberal capitalist democracies, however, attitudes in those two sets of roles remain distinct, and a central elite strategy in such systems involves the maintenance of that "distance" between political opinions and the attitudes of the subject population in class and status roles. Thus, it is possible for significant inequalities in income distribution, for instance, to go hand in hand with relative egalitarianism in "citizen" roles. As the discussion below on authority relations points out again, the task of coping with this apparent contradiction requires the exercise by the modern state of a formidable array of techniques for social control, socialization, legitimation, and coercion.

POLITICAL STRUCTURE

The political structure is the elite apparatus for decision-making, and in the United States it includes Presidents, congressmen, judges in the appellate courts, some members of the executive branch, and some interest group leaders. The political structure is affected by stimuli from the three external sources outlined above. Its members seek to formulate policy responses that will protect their own incumbency interests as well as the regime structure itself. In response to some types of disturbances, the political structure itself undergoes change. Thus, Mansfield, Price, and Polsby have all described changing patterns of institutionalization in Congress,[19] and Cronin has provided data on the growth of staff agencies in the presidency.[20] Scattered attempts have also been made to develop quantitative measures of changing relationships between institutions within the political structure. Fisher has pointed out that changes in the distribution of treaties and executive agreements might be a rough indicator of shifts in influence over foreign relations between Congress and the presidency; and Funston has shown that conflict between the Supreme Court and Congress rises during realignment eras.[21]

Decades ago, as political science struggled to move beyond legalistic and formalistic questions about political institutions, some scholars simply chose to ignore formal institutions, arguing that they were at worst epiphenomenal and at best dependent variables in any serious study of politics. But institutional arrangements can and do have an independent influence on other political variables. Robert Michels showed how organizations develop their own goals and interests, and students of bureaucratic politics continue to point to the importance of such factors in political decision-making.[22] Both Huntington and Burnham deduce consequences (incorrectly, I believe) about political development from institutional arrangements within the national government. And James S. Young's chronicle of the early years of political life in the new capital of Washington vividly demonstrates how organizational theory and ideas and concepts about government can be translated into structure, and in turn how important the influence of structure is on the behavior of the occupants of political roles. The structural constraints imposed by the Constitution on the new governors of the United States were remarkably successful in limiting and even subverting the power of the national government, and the exercise of substantial power from the seat of government in Washington had to await development of a number of extra-constitutional devices, like the creation of a structured party apparatus in Congress, before a working system of political leadership could survive.[23]

In short, changes in the formal structure of political organizations may often reflect changes in other political variables, just as changes in institutional configuration may sometimes stimulate changes in other regime components. In either case, indicators of change in the regime's political structure must be part of any comprehensive study of political change and development.

FOREIGN RELATIONS

If sources of disturbance external to the regime itself often impinge on its activities, it follows that the political elite will seek to develop policies and agencies to control and stabilize relationships with those disruptive elements. One set of policies involves foreign relations, those state activities which regulate and control interaction with the international environment. Inputs required to carry out this task generally involve information—intelligence about the military, diplomatic, and economic activities of other nations and international organizations. Outputs are the military, diplomatic, economic, and immigration policies adopted to maintain or increase control over the international environment.

As a regime develops more or less differentiated strategies for dealing with each source of external disturbance, it also develops a more or less differentiated apparatus for carrying out those policies. For the conduct of foreign relations in the United States, this apparatus includes the armed forces, intelligence agencies, and the State Department and diplomatic corps. Other, less obvious participants in the maintenance of foreign relations are business corporations, who sometimes provide information to decision-makers and personnel to carry out foreign policies (see the American electronic installation in the Sinai desert); and the mass media, who are an important and timely source of foreign intelligence and often serve as unofficial propaganda agents abroad (see, for example, the international editions of *Time* or *Newsweek*).

ALLOCATIVE RELATIONS

From an elite perspective, relationships with the nation's technoeconomic base are as crucial as foreign relations, and a distinguishable set of policies involves state activities to control and support that base. On the input side, the regime must guarantee a flow of revenues adequate to pay for all of its activities (including defense and social control). As the preceding cases have demonstrated, the creation of an adequate extractive system is often a difficult problem for a new regime. On the output side, allocative policies include what James O'Connor has called the creation of social capital,[24] control of labor relations, support for crucial industrial sectors, and macroeconomic regulation. Such policies generally aim at maintenance of the existing economic system, but not because the political elite is "the executive committee of the ruling class." Rather, a regime's extractive system must be designed to fit carefully with a nation's economic base, and if the nation's economy collapses, so must the state's revenue flow. If a nation's economic base is radically transformed, the regime's extractive system must be rebuilt to match.

In the United States, the agents involved in carrying out these allocative tasks are federal bureaucracies (including regulatory commissions), the courts, and interest groups. Unrecognized but nonetheless crucial is the role that corporations perform in the process of extraction. Businesses and other corporate entities provide the apparatus to collect most personal income taxes through withholding, a device which has made tax rebellions almost impossible. (At the local level, retail merchants also collect sales taxes for state and municipal governments.)

As a rule, the elite seeks to maintain some rough correspondence between in- and outflows of funds, and unless extraordinary circumstances are present, those revenues must be extracted from the subject population in the form of taxes. Once in a while, high levels of profits from imperialistic ventures in other countries or the proceeds from booty collected in warfare may spare the citizenry from high levels of internal resource extraction, and still provide the elite with adequate levels of funds to carry out its objectives. Alternatively, some extraordinary cache of natural resources, like South Africa's huge stock of gold and diamonds or Libya's great pools of oil, may provide the political apparatus with adequate levels of concrete resources. More often, such sources contribute a relatively small share of the revenues necessary for elite support, and the bulk of those resources must be collected from the citizens of the system, in the form of taxes or special grants of manpower.

Disputes over regime strategies for maintaining adequate flows of revenues are easy enough to find; the debate over the impost under the Articles of Confederation was one such argument. Moreover, it is simple to calculate the political consequences suffered by a regime which is unable to assure some rough balance between its inputs and its expenditures. If outputs exceed inputs, regime activities must be cut back. If the elite is fortunate enough to have a surplus to work with, it may seek to expand its control over the subject population or the internatonal environment, or it may, as Warren Ilchman and Norman Uphoff suggest, undertake some "investments" in political or administrative infrastructure or in programs designed to build stability, legitimacy, or solidarity.[25] Alternatively, the elite may reduce the extractive burden on the population, hoping to build good will in that fashion. In practice, the issue of a surplus does not often arise. During Jefferson's presidency, he and Gallatin struggled valiantly with the problem of how to use the surplus projected after the debt was paid off. The Embargo solved the problem by eliminating the surplus.

In return for its grant of resources, the elite must usually convince its subjects that regime activities are in some way necessary or valuable to them if the population at large is not to feel exploited. What Barrington Moore said about Chinese villages seems applicable to all political systems: "The thesis put forward here merely holds that the contributions of those who fight, rule, and pray must be obvious to the peasant, and the peasants' return payments must not be grossly out of proportion to the services received." If that is not the case, Moore argues that a situation of "objective exploitation" exists.[26]

An equally pertinent issue is the extent to which individual citizens or members of discrete groups believe that the particularistic benefits they receive are roughly equivalent to their payments in support of the regime. The correspondence between the beneficiaries of government outputs and those who pay for its costs is highly problematic. It is by no means certain, for example, that those sectors which pay out the largest amounts of revenues will in turn receive the largest benefits from state action. Murry Edelman argues that the relationship is often quite the opposite, and that members of the mass public—who pay the largest amounts of taxes— usually receive only symbolic benefits in return, while corporate bodies, like business and interest groups—whose payments are smaller—receive the largest distributive benefits.[27] Alternatively, members of the white middle and lower middle class in cities often argue that they pay the most taxes, but that blacks and other minorities receive a disproportionate share of benefits. They believe, perhaps correctly, that government distributes those rewards in an effort to maintain quiescence, not as returns to those who pay the costs. Whatever the merits of either of those arguments—and they cannot be adequately assessed without more and better data on allocative activities—it is clear that there is no necessary correspondence between contributors of revenues and recipients of benefits, and it is certainly possible that the relationship is a negative one.

An historical example illustrates the scope of the problem and the need for more analysis in this area. During the 1790s, farmers and Southerners frequently complained that they were being exploited, as Barrington Moore used the term, because they paid most of the taxes and the merchants and men of commerce received most of the benefits under the Federalist administrations. Indeed, the merchants did profit from new commercial treaties and from the navy's protection, and the "monied interest" reaped the rewards from Hamilton's plan for funding and assumption. Although those well-to-do people also consumed large amounts of imported luxury items and, therefore, paid heavy tariff duties, it is still unlikely that their payments in dollars were proportionate to their share of concrete benefits under the new regime.

But the political elite wanted more than just taxes from the merchants and bankers and new industrialists; they wanted other kinds of support as well. Those groups bought bonds and lent money to the government. They provided much of its personnel. They provided the main apparatus for tax collection, since merchants paid tariff duties in lump sums when goods were imported, and collected the revenues piecemeal from the general population at point of sale. Thus, some correspondence between the regime's needs and the distribution of its rewards is apparent, but the relationship is complex, and the charge that the South and the countryside were in some objective sense exploited cannot be refuted.

AUTHORITY RELATIONS

Finally, the maintenance of stable or increasing levels of control over the subject population in its "citizen" roles is a central task for any regime, as rulers seek to assure compliance in authority relations. To perform this task, the elite requires a wide range of information about its subjects. It uses that data to make rough predictions about how often compliance will be voluntary and how often coercion will be needed; which commands might provoke resistance; and from which population sectors such resistance might arise. A society's technological sophistication is an important limitation on the quality of these inputs. For instance, in the period under study in my case studies, mail between cities took weeks instead of days for delivery, and newspapers were infrequent, small in size, and restricted in circulation. Under such circumstances, the information available to the elite for assessment of mass attitudes was much more limited than at present, when electronic communication media and sophisticated analysis by social scientists provide more reliable techniques for gauging citizen support.

Inputs which assist the elite in carrying out the tasks of social control and legitimation may include data about voting and nonvoting, attitudes toward the government, and intelligence about social movements, protest groups, and civil and criminal disobedience.

David Easton uses the perfectly sensible term, "demands," to describe a number of these categories of data. As I suggested earlier, it is indeed satisfying from the point of view of democratic theory to postulate that demands from groups and citizens must play a crucial role in determining elite actions. In this formulation, however, demands are just another set of data about citizen attitudes, another indicator—and usually a positive one—about support levels. Just as most of a child's demands on its parents are an indication of its affection toward and dependence upon them, so I assume that most political demands—more specifically, demands for normal outputs which can be met without alteration of the regime—are also an indication of positive affective attachment and general support for an existing regime. On the other hand, demands for regime alteration are negative indicators of support levels, and as such constitute an important warning signal to political actors seeking to maintain an existing regime structure. For my own purposes, I find it difficult to distinguish demands from supports, and I will therefore lump them all together under the broader description of "compliance predictors."

With data in hand on citizens' attitudes, the elite may undertake a wide range of activities to assure adequate levels of compliance, including the direct use of coercive force, more subtle strategies of socialization and legitimation, or the dispensation of concrete benefits. To discuss these activities is to discuss "authority," a term used in several different and ambiguous ways in political analysis. Once in a while, the word is used in its most restricted sense, to connote expertise; thus, Henry Kissinger is an authority on foreign relations. Easton also uses the term in a special sense to designate the occupants of elite political roles, whom he calls "the authorities." But most often, the word is used in one way or another to describe the relationship between command and compliance. Authority is sometimes seen as the "right" to command, an attribute of the dominant member in a command relationship. In that sense, the term is often linked with *legitimacy*, which is instead a special reason why subordinates obey—because they sometimes believe that compliance is a duty, and that they "ought" to obey their rulers' commands.*

But there are several different reasons why a subordinate may obey a command. Indeed, a command may be seen as legitimate, and obeyed for that reason. Or, since most state commands are backed up by force and the threat of punishment, the citizen may obey because of fear of the consequences of disobedience. Or obedience may be "purchased" through some distributive activity of the state; [28] James Scott indicates that particularistic distribution is the main base for compliance in systems where "machine politics" prevails.[29] Or obedience may be habitual, based on many years of past compliance with similar commands. Max Weber's comments on staff obedience to rulers' commands seem equally applicable to the analysis of mass compliance:"It is understood that, in reality, obedience is determined by highly robust motives of fear and hope—fear of the vengeance of magical powers or of the power-holder, hope for reward in this world or in the beyond—and besides all this, by interests of the most varied sort." [30]

Political rulers recognize these varied bases for compliance, and in support of any given command put to use a variety of techniques to assure compliance at whatever level they believe is necessary. Usually an enforcement staff is created to bring coercive sanctions to bear against those who disobey. Occasionally what James O'Connor calls "social expenses" are dispensed,[31] in the form of rewards (like welfare payments) to assure mass compliance. Other concrete benefits, like tax loopholes or direct subsidies, are sometimes provided to corporate groups. Moreover, as Murray Edelman has pointed out,[32] a wide variety of symbolic activities usually accompany new commands, from flag-waving to careful ideological justification of an order.

---

* It is sometimes hard to remember that a citizen may accept a command as legitimate and recognize his or her duty to obey it, but still may refuse to comply with that command, if the costs of compliance outweigh the rewards of doing one's duty. See Young, *The Washington Community*, p. 229, for example.

The elite need not necessarily know or care which of these techniques elicits compliance from any given citizen (except, as noted below, when the costs of these techniques are different), nor necessarily care whether any single citizen obeys any specific command. Their concern is with the maintenance of an overall level of compliance, given the array of techniques available to them, and when that effort is successful, they believe quite correctly that they have established their authority. So from the perspective of the elite, "authority" suggests not simply a set of moral injunctions about right to command or duty to obey, but can be understood more generally as a "probablistic judgment or prediction about the likelihood of compliance by subordinates."[33] The term will be so used in this essay.

States differ in their applications of authority, and distinctions can be drawn along at least two dimensions. On the one hand, totalitarian regimes can be distinguished from other states because of the higher *level* of authoritative control exercised. On the other hand, regimes also differ in their choice of *patterns of domination,* the characteristic mix of coercive, distributive, and legitimating techniques employed to maintain the desired level of compliance. (Habit triggers, like traffic lights and subway turnstiles, are also an available tool, but they will be ignored in the discussion which follows.)

Over the long run, welfare states and "machine" systems tend to settle on distributive activities in support of their commands. In *Regulating the Poor,*[34] Piven and Cloward show that distribution (of welfare grants and poor relief, for instance) can be an effective short-run strategy for reestablishing or maintaining quiescence. By definition, repressive or "police" states use high levels of coercion to maintain compliance. But in some states like Great Britain, where deference to authority is well-established in the political culture, coercive activities are less evident, and the symbolic and ideological activities of legitimation seem sufficient to assure authority.

Max Weber, of course, went even further, and attempted a typology of legitimation, based on the citizen-based inner justifications to which state activity was directed; he pointed to the timeless authority of tradition, the personal authority of the charismatic leader, and the rational authority of legality.[35] A number of contemporary social scientists still think that types of legitimation are useful criteria for classifying regimes. For example, in his discussion of authority patterns in West Africa, Aristide Zolberg states that: "Systems can then be characterized as clusterings of legitimacy variables, and it would be possible to understand how the salience of these types of beliefs can vary over time within the same system denoting important changes at the level of the regime." [36] Indeed, classification using those criteria might well be useful, so long as it is clear that what is changing are elite strategies and techniques, and so long as that classification is preceded by a prior determination of the place of legitimation in the overall pattern of domination.

Thus in the first decades of the American polity, the nature of appeals for voluntary compliance to taxes and other commands underwent a striking shift. Because political institutions were new and obviously man-made, the appeal to tradition—which had been useful under the monarchy—had to be abandoned. For a few brief years, George Washington's charismatic appeal helped to shore up state authority. [37] But at the same time, Hamilton and others were trying to build a "rational" case for state authority and justify taxes with arguments about public credit. The Federalists in general and Hamilton in particular were also quite willing to use what coercive force was available to the young state. They used troops and courts against the whiskey rebels and the tiny band of tax resisters in Bucks County, and the Alien and Sedition Acts against opponents during the near war with France.

In modern liberal democracies, legitimating strategies invariably include a series of devices for involving mass publics in the choice of some segment of the political elite. The political party is therefore a key agent in the maintenance of authority relations in such regimes. Other groups which carry out these tasks in America include the courts, police and other bureaucracies (spanning the spectrum from HEW to the military), the mass media, and interest groups.

For many students of political development, an unquestioned assumption is that a highly developed state is centralized and well differentiated, with specialized institutions performing specialized functions. In my listing of the private and public agencies which perform these tasks in the United States, there is substantial overlap from function to function. The mass media, interest groups, corporations, and a wide range of bureaucracies appear on several of those lists. In addition, the political structure is decentralized in America, retaining a bicameral legislature and a constitutional doctrine of "separation of powers." Some scholars therefore conclude that America is still an underdeveloped polity.

However, the data presented in chapter 1 suggest that the central state apparatus in the United States exercises sizable levels of control which have increased over the years. Moreover, in America, the work of the regime does get done. New citizens are socialized and noncompliants punished. Taxes are collected and sophisticated macroeconomic policies implemented. America's influence is felt throughout the international state system. Indeed, contrary to the conventional wisdom, elite control in the United States is all the more secure, precisely because these tasks are carried out by multipurpose, largely undifferentiated agencies, and the subject population is therefore far less likely to realize the scope and nature of state control. A centralized and rationalized state apparatus might perform these tasks with slightly greater efficiency, but the extent of its control would inevitably be easier to grasp than at present. In "Class, Status and Party," Max Weber argues that the "transparency" of class inequalities, or the extent to which members of a subordinate class recognize their class position, in large part determines the likelihood that such groups will act to overthrow the rule of a dominant class.[38] In the same way, to the extent that decentralization and lack of differentiation within the American regime reduce the "transparency" of state control, the likelihood that subordinate members of the subject population will act to overthrow their political rulers is also substantially reduced.

STUDYING REGIME CHANGE

Although the preceding analysis has been presented at a rather abstract level, the problem of finding operational indicators for the variables discussed in this chapter is not so difficult as it might appear at first glance. Because of America's relatively long history as a nation, its generally high level of skill in record-keeping, and the strenuous efforts of historians and social scientists, data sets are available that might serve as indicators of change in many of these regime components. Although any single data set might be less than perfectly reliable, it is usually possible to suggest several indicators for each variable; the strategy of using multiple indicators is costly in terms of data collection. However, it guards against the problem of unreliability in any isolated set of data, and also permits analysis of the multidimensional character of each of these components.

Data is available on sources of disturbance external to the regime. For example, economic historians have labored long and hard to reconstruct valid indices for measuring historical changes in America's technoeconomic base, and longitudinal data exist on many aspects of economic transformation for the period from 1870 to the present.[39] Data on demographic change drawn from the census and other sources are also available. Moreover, political scientists have assembled longitudinal data on mass political behavior. The growing banks of survey data cover too brief a time period to be of much value in the kind of analysis proposed here. But the Interuniversity Consortium for Political Research at the University of Michigan has made available data on aggregate voting patterns and an interesting (if somewhat problematic) set of data on political violence.[40] Both sets of data stretch back past the Civil War. Disturbances in the international environment are much harder to measure, but for exploratory research, it might be sufficient to construct a scale which distinguishes between war, near war (the late 1790s and the cold war, for example), and the absence of war.

Measures of change in the political structure can be constructed from data on workload, staff size, recruitment patterns, and voting coalitions for both Congress and the appellate courts. For the period from 1939 to the present, data on staff growth in the presidency would also be of value. Budget figures are available specifying the amount of money spent on the activities of each institution, although Presidents often "borrow" staff and other valuable resources from line agencies and do not include such exchanges in their staff budgets. It should also be possible to develop indicators of levels of conflict between institutions, using presidential vetoes and congressional overrides, rejected nominations, or rejections by the Supreme Court of congressional legislation.[41]

For indicators of changes in foreign, allocative, and authority relations, measures of the personnel and funds expended in each of those areas would be the most important requirement. Except for recent years, when restrictions have been placed on information about the secret activities of intelligence agencies, it is reasonably simple to determine from budgets how much money is spent on foreign as opposed to domestic activities and what percentage of federal personnel are employed in those activities.

Data on sources of revenues (both by geographical area and by type of tax) are also available in the government's own reports and accounts.

Finally, as suggested earlier, it is possible to suggest summary indicators of changes in state capacity. The percentage of gross national product allocated to state activities, and the percentage of the population directly employed by the government are useful, if quite crude, indicators of changes in state capacity.

One operational problem resists easy solution. Without much more detailed analysis of policies and of the activities of federal bureaucracies, it is difficult indeed to distinguish expenditures and personnel employed in social control from those employed in allocative activities. In many cases, the same bureaucratic units carry out both sets of activities, and neither line nor program budgets are designed to help political scientists analyze state authority. Moreover, in the United States, much of the work of social control and socialization is carried out by state and local governments, whose budgets and records are dispersed and difficult to summarize.

Until that problem is solved, many of the finer questions raised by this paradigm cannot be answered. It is still impossible to determine, for instance, whether distribution or coercion is a more costly basis for assuring compliance. The question is a complex one. In a modern welfare state, expensive rewards—which, as Piven and Cloward point out, can be used to assure compliance—must be given to every citizen within general categories established by law, even those who might comply with state commands quite voluntarily. Coercion, on the other hand, is applied only against the residual category of citizens who refuse to obey commands. While this argument suggests that a repressive state might be cheaper to run than a welfare state, the equation is still too simple. Heavy applications of coercion often weaken the voluntary base for compliance, and diminish state legitimacy. When the British stepped up enforcements efforts in Boston after passage of the Townshend Acts, they alienated the colonial population even further. Coercion may, therefore, have long-run costs that are not immediately apparent to decision-makers.

Without indicators capable of very precise measurement, research questions at this level of complexity cannot be answered, but with data sets like those outlined above, covering time periods of sufficient length (perhaps fifty years and up), a number of hypotheses about patterns of change in different regime components could be tested. I have argued, for instance, that one widespread (if often unspoken) assumption about political change in the United States is that it occurs in small increments. (For analytic purposes, it might be more sensible to consider incrementalism as a strategy used by the political elite to turn back proposals for more radical changes, and then try to discover the circumstances under which that strategy succeeds or fails.) Burnham, on the other hand, has pointed out nonincremental changes in voting behavior, and has argued that this pattern of sharp, periodic transformation might also describe behavior in the national policy agenda and the political structure.[42] Studies by Funston and Ginsberg present evidence that realignments do have some impact on levels of conflict between institutions and on policy shifts.[43] Finch and I have used interrupted time series analysis to argue that a third pattern of change is evident in American politics, consisting of nonincremental developmental increases in allocative indicators, resulting from wars.[44]

Further analysis of indicators of change in all the regime variables suggested in Figure 6.1 would indicate the extent to which various regime components have changed according to these distinctive patterns, and would also help to identify the sources and rough magnitudes of the stimuli which provoke those changes. I have already pointed out one example: Burnham suggests—but offers no data to prove—that periodic realignments are related to changes in the socioeconomic base in America. Such hypotheses demand testing. Finally, analysis of longitudinal changes in regime indicators might also help identify the ways in which one regime component interacts with other components. Wars transform allocative indicators, but also can either dampen popular protest, or provoke draft riots and resistance. Ginsberg argues that realignments transform policy outputs;[45] that effect should be visible in changing allocative indicators as well as changing policy agendas. And in general, the kind of analysis proposed here might help specify the boundary conditions under which such diverse effects and interactions occur.

CONCLUSION

In chapter 5, I argued that it is sometimes helpful to group political events in America into four large categories: normal politics, two kinds of crisis politics, and regime politics. Most political scientists in the United States spend their time studying normal politics, and there are excellent reasons to continue such study. Without some understanding of who participates and who is denied access, who benefits and who loses, and how choices are made in normal politics, it is impossible to make sense of government and politics in contemporary America. Crisis politics is an equally worthwhile candidate for study. If a crisis is an occasion when some grave threat to the functioning of the regime is present, then the skill with which the elite manages such situations can determine in some sense whether a political system will live or die.

But the central focus of this essay has been regime politics and regime change, and its central purpose has been to advocate further study of political change and development in the United States. In the study of other nations, political scientists have showed their concern for these issues, but their curiosity rarely seems to extend to the United States. If they hesitate because authority crises (which are the most obvious indicators of unrest and change) are so rare in this nation, I have tried to indicate in these case studies that significant change in a regime can take place without an authority crisis, a pattern that seems the rule and not the exception in the United States. Moreover, in Figure 6.1, I have suggested one set of variables that might be used to study such transformation. The task is difficult. America's political history is long and complex, and over the past two hundred years vast quantities of data of varying usefulness have accumulated. But the end-product of such analysis is simply too valuable to ignore: a clearer understanding of patterns of political change throughout the history of the United States, and a much firmer base for speculation about the changing shape of American politics in the future.

/ NOTES

1 / TAXATION AND REGIME CHANGE: AN INTRODUCTION

1. Tilly, ed., *Formation of National States.*

2. *Ibid.*, pp. 164–327.

3. *Ibid.*, pp. 96–97.

4. Easton, *Systems Analysis of Political Life*, p. 190.

5. Mosca, *Ruling Class*, pp. 70–71.

6. See, for example, Elton, *Tudor Constitution;* or Williams, *Eighteenth-Century Constitution.*

7. Greenstone and Peterson, *Race and Authority in Urban Politics*, esp. ch. 4.

8. Easton, *Systems Analysis of Political Life*, p. 191.

9. Pye and Verba, eds., *Political Culture and Political Development*, p. 513.

10. *Ibid.*, p. 516.

11. Singer, *General Systems Taxonomy*, p. 9.

12. *Ibid.*, p. 8.

13. Hartz, *Liberal Tradition in America*, p. 7.

14. *Ibid.*, p. 9.

15. Huntington, *Political Order in Changing Societies*, p. 130.

16. *Ibid.*, p. 98.

17. See, for instance, Burnham, *Critical Elections;* or MacRae and Meldrum, "Critical Elections in Illinois."

18. Burnham, *Critical Elections*, p. 91.

19. Lowi, *American Government: Incomplete Conquest*, p. 10 (his italics).

20. Young, *Washington Community*, p. 29; *Statistical Abstract*, pp. 5, 243; *Budget of the U.S. Government*, pp. 13, 71; *Historical Statistics*, p. 139.

21. Finch and Forsythe, "Theories of American Political Change."

2 / MONEY, THE "INDISPENSABLE INGREDIENT"

1. Lipset, *First New Nation;* Jensen, *New Nation.*

2. *Federalist,* p. 188.

3. Ferguson, *Power of the Purse,* p. 290.

4. Dickerson, *Navigation Acts,* pp. 31 ff.

5. *Ibid.,* p. 173.

6. Morgan, *Birth of the Republic,* p. 17.

7. *Ibid.,* pp. 25–26.

8. *Ibid.,* pp. 30–31.

9. Dickerson, *Navigation Acts,* pp. 52–53, 300; Miller, *Origins of the American Revolution,* p. 89.

10. Wright, *Fabric of Freedom,* pp. 100–1.

11. Lowi, *American Government: Incomplete Conquest,* p. 4.

12. Barnard, *Functions of the Executive,* p. 167.

13. Morgan, *Birth of the Republic,* p. 20.

14. Page Smith, "David Ramsay and the Causes of the American Revolution," p. 54; see also p. 59.

15. Ferguson, *Power of the Purse,* pp. 111–12.

16. Duane to Washington, Jan. 29, 1781, quoted in Jensen, *New Nation,* pp. 54–55.

17. Ferguson, *Power of the Purse,* p. 142.

18. *Ibid.,* p. 117.

19. *Ibid.,* p. 154.

20. *Ibid.,* pp. 147, 143.

21. April 30, 1781, quoted in Jensen, *New Nation,* p. 45.

22. Ferguson, *Power of the Purse,* p. 149.

23. *Ibid.,* pp. 147–51.

24. Jensen, *New Nation,* p. 64.

25. Ferguson, *Power of the Purse,* pp. 160, 166.

26. *Ibid.,* pp. 156–57.

27. *Ibid.,* p. 160.

28. Feb. 7, 1789, quoted in Jensen, *New Nation,* p. 71.

29. Ferguson, *Power of the Purse,* pp. 162–63.

30. Jensen, *New Nation,* pp. 75–76; and Ferguson, *Power of the Purse,* pp. 166–67.

31. Unless otherwise noted, this and other information on reactions in the states has been drawn from Jensen, *New Nation,* pp. 411–17.

32. *Ibid.,* p. 417.

33. Beard, *Economic Interpretation of the Constitution,* p. 176.

34. *Ibid.,* pp. 169–70.

35. Farrand, *Records,* 1:284.

36. *Ibid.,* 1:305.

37. *Federalist,* #27, p. 176.

38. The quotation is from White, *Federalists,* p. 411; other pertinent information is found in the same work at p. 117, and in White, *Jeffersonians,* pp. 148–49.

39. Morris, ed., *Hamilton and the Founding of the Nation,* p. 240.

40. *Federalist,* #32, p. 199.

41. Sept. 26, 1787, quoted in Ferguson, *Power of the Purse,* p. 292.

42. *Federalist,* #36, p. 221.

43. *Federalist,* #12, p. 92–93.

44. *Federalist,* #30, p. 190; #34, p. 208.

45. *American State Papers: Finance,* 1:665.

46. Ferguson, *Power of the Purse,* p. 341.

47. *Ibid.,* p. 301.

48. *Ibid.,* p. 307.

49. Miller, *Federalist Era,* p. 46.

50. Ferguson, *Power of the Purse,* pp. 310–11.

51. Cooke, ed., *Reports of Hamilton,* pp. 48, 50, 51.

52. Miller, *Hamilton,* p. 262.

53. Cooke, ed., *Reports of Hamilton,* p. xviii.

54. For a fuller picture of the incident, see Miller, *Hamilton,* pp. 263–67.

55. Cooke, ed., *Reports of Hamilton,* p. 2.

56. *Ibid.,* pp. 5, 23.

57. Miller, *Hamilton,* p. 253; Bruchey, *Roots of American Economic Growth,* pp. 110–11.

58. Cooke, ed., *Reports of Hamilton,* p. 4.

59. *An Inquiry into the Principles and Policy of the Government of the United States,* quoted in Beard, *Economic Origins of Jeffersonian Democracy,* p. 331.

60. Weber, *Theory of Social and Economic Organization,* p. 328.

61. White, *Federalists,* p. 404.

62. *Ibid.,* p. 404 (fn).

63. *Federalist,* #17, p. 120.

64. Rossiter, *Hamilton and the Constitution,* pp. 135–36.

65. Beard, *Economic Origins of Jeffersonian Democracy,* p. 246.

66. Miller, *Hamilton,* pp. 311–12.

67. Ferguson, *Power of the Purse,* p. 342.

68. *Federalist,* #10, p. 79.

69. Dauer, *Adams Federalists,* p. 4.

70. Malone, *Jefferson,* 2:338.

71. Beard, *Economic Origins of Jeffersonian Democracy,* p. 138.

72. *Ibid.,* pp. 122–24.

73. Miller, *Hamilton,* p. 272.

74. *Ibid.,* p. 311.

75. *Ibid.,* p. 285.

76. *Ibid.,* p. 255.

77. Miller, *Federalist Era,* p. 41.

78. Miller, *Hamilton,* pp. 268–69.

3 / INTERNAL TAXES

1. U.S. Continental Congress, *Journals,* 1:109, quoted in Baldwin, *Whiskey Rebels,* p. 63; see also pp. 23–25. Throughout this section on the Whiskey Rebellion, I rely heavily on Baldwin's excellent monograph.

2. *Johnson's Dictionary,* ed. by E. L. McAdam Jr. and George Milne, p. 170.

3. Morris, *Hamilton and the Founding of the Nation,* p. 331.

4. Cooke, ed., *Reports of Hamilton,* p. 34.

5. White, *Federalists,* pp. 200–01; Baldwin, *Whiskey Rebels,* p. 68.

6. Baldwin, *Whiskey Rebels,* pp. 26–28.

7. Miller, *Hamilton,* pp. 396–97.

8. Baldwin, *Whiskey Rebels,* p. 71.

9. Beard, *Economic Origins of Jeffersonian Democracy,* p. 252.

10. Bruchey, *Roots of American Growth,* p. 112.

11. Baldwin, *Whiskey Rebels*, p. 28.
12. Ferguson, *Power of the Purse*, p. 318.
13. Beard, *Economic Origins of Jeffersonian Democracy*, p. 251.
14. Baldwin, *Whiskey Rebels*, p. 67.
15. Mitchell, *Hamilton*, 2:316.
16. Baldwin, Whiskey Rebels, pp. 72, 110–11.
17. Merritt, *Symbols of American Community*, p. 20.
18. Miller, *Federalist Era*, p. 2.
19. Baldwin, *Whiskey Rebels*, p. 105.
20. Morris, ed., *Hamilton and the Founding of the Nation*, pp. 105–06.
21. Baldwin, *Whiskey Rebels*, pp. 105–06.
22. Walters, *Gallatin*, pp. 69–70.
23. Baldwin, *Whiskey Rebels*, p. 112.
24. *Ibid.*, pp. 103, 170.
25. Miller, *Federalist Era*, p. 159.
26. See Baldwin, *Whiskey Rebels*, for a full description of each incident.
27. *Ibid.*, pp. 206–8.
28. Woodbury, *Public Opinion in Philadelphia*, p. 115.
29. Baldwin, *Whiskey Rebels*, pp. 183–85; Miller, *Hamilton*, p. 407.
30. March 18, 1799, Hamilton to J. McHenry, in Morris, ed., *Hamilton and the Founding of the Nation*, p. 492.
31. Baldwin, *Whiskey Rebels*, p. 112 (his italics).
32. *Ibid.*, pp. 11–12.
33. Miller, *Hamilton*, pp. 405–9.
34. Baldwin, *Whiskey Rebels*, pp. 209–15.
35. *Ibid.*, pp. 217, 228–29.
36. *Ibid.*, pp. 253, 258, 263–64.
37. Balinky, *Gallatin*, pp. 36, 61–62.
38. Walters, *Gallatin*, p. 148.
39. Morris, ed., *Hamilton and the Founding of the Nation*, pp. 333–35; Malone, *Jefferson*, 3:99.
40. Morris, ed., *Hamilton and the Founding of the Nation*, p. 341.
41. *Ibid.*, p. 329.
42. Dauer, *Adams Federalists*, pp. 128–29, 137.
43. *Ibid.*, pp. 145–46.
44. Kurtz, *Presidency of John Adams*, p. 309.
45. Miller, *Federalist Era*, pp. 212, 210–12.
46. Walters, *Gallatin*, p. 110.
47. White, *Federalists*, p. 206.
48. Dauer, *Adams Federalists*, p. 168.
49. Kurtz, *Presidency of John Adams*, p. 321.
50. Chambers, *Political Parties in the New Nation*, p. 140.
51. Kurtz, *Presidency of John Adams*, p. 363.
52. *Ibid.*, p. 359.
53. Beard, *Economic Origins of Jeffersonian Democracy*, p. 215 (italics in the original).
54. Adams, *Taxation in the U.S.*, p. 57; Kurtz, *Presidency of John Adams*, p. 361.
55. Davis, *Fries Rebellion*, p. 37.
56. *Ibid.*, pp. 68–71.
57. *Ibid.*, p. 139.

58. *Ibid.*, p. 133.
59. Walters, *Gallatin*, p. 121.
60. Balinky, *Gallatin*, p. viii.
61. *Ibid.*, pp. 62–63.
62. *Ibid.*, p. 90.
63. Walters, *Gallatin*, p. 209.
64. Balinky, *Gallatin*, p. 38.
65. Brown, *Republic in Peril*, p. 35.
66. Balinky, *Gallatin*, pp. 179–80.
67. Smelser, *Democratic Republic*, pp. 286, 232.
68. Adams, *Taxation in the U.S.*, p. 58; Balinky, *Gallatin*, p. 16.
69. Adams, *Taxation in the U.S.*, p. 67.
70. Brown, *Republic in Peril.*

4 / THE TARIFF

1. Woodbury, *Public Opinion in Philadelphia*, p. 36.
2. Stanwood, *American Tariff Controversies*, 1:53.
3. *Ibid.*, 1:44.
4. Miller, *Federalist Era*, p. 16.
5. Stanwood, *American Tariff Controversies*, 1:61–62.
6. White, *Federalists*, p. 464; see also pp. 460–65.
7. Adams, *Taxation in the U.S.*, p. 64.
8. Fish, *Civil Service and Patronage*, p. 11.
9. White, *Federalists*, pp. 6, 304–8; Walters, *Gallatin*, p. 144.
10. White, *Federalists*, p. 515.
11. *Ibid.*, pp. 468–69; White, *Jeffersonians*, pp. 138–39.
12. Stanwood, *American Tariff Controversies*, 1:111.
13. Dangerfield, *Awakening of American Nationalism*, p. 14.
14. Wiltse, *Calhoun*, 1:122.
15. Dangerfield, *Awakening of American Nationalism*, p. 6.
16. *Ibid.*, p. 140.
17. Current, *Webster*, p. 22.
18. Coit, *Calhoun*, p. 113; also Stanwood, *American Tariff Controversies*, 1:152.
19. Wiltse, *Calhoun*, 1:404 (retabulated).
20. Stanwood, *American Tariff Controversies*, 1:157–58.
21. Wiltse, *Calhoun*, 1:120.
22. Dangerfield, *Awakening of American Nationalism*, p. 16.
23. Taussig, *Tariff History*, p. 68.
24. Stanwood, *American Tariff Controversies*, 1:189–90.
25. Current, *Webster*, p. 36.
26. Stanwood, *American Tariff Controversies*, 1:190 (fn).
27. *Ibid.*, 1:190.
28. Current, *Webster*, p. 35.
29. Sydnor, *Southern Sectionalism*, pp. 31–32.
30. *Ibid.*, pp. 127–28.
31. *Historical Statistics*, p. 13.
32. Sydnor, *Southern Sectionalism*, p. 139.
33. Wiltse, *Calhoun*, 1:287.
34. Stanwood, *American Tariff Controversies*, 1:202–4.

35. *Ibid.*, p. 221.

36. Wiltse, *Calhoun*, 1:288; Dangerfield, *Awakening of American Nationalism*, pp. 204–5.

37. Dangerfield, *Awakening of American Nationalism*, p. 237.

38. Taussig, *Tariff History*, p. 75.

39. Dangerfield, *Awakening of American Nationalism*, p. 237.

40. *Ibid.*, p. 205.

41. Current, *Webster*, p. 40.

42. Freehling, *Prelude to Civil War*, pp. 119–20. I have relied on this excellent study throughout this section on the tariff from 1828 to 1833.

43. Taussig, *Tariff History*, pp. 78–79.

44. Freehling, ed., *Nullification Era*, pp. 126–28.

45. *Ibid.*, p. 37.

46. *Ibid.*, p. 21.

47. *Ibid.*, p. 25.

48. Stanwood, *American Tariff Controversies*, 1:261.

49. *Ibid.*, p. 262.

50. Freehling, ed., *Nullification Era*, pp. 104–19.

51. See Taussig, *Tariff History*, pp. 95–96; Wiltse, *Calhoun*, 1:368; Stanwood, *American Tariff Controversies*, 1:271, and others. However, Robert V. Remini has offered an alternative to this standard interpretation of the committee bill. He suggests that Van Buren hoped that the bill would succeed, and that it might help bring new support into the Jacksonian camp. Van Buren was certain that the South would never support Adams, Remini says, and thought that the high tariffs on such items as raw wool and iron and hemp might entice the Western and Middle states into supporting Jackson. Remini also points to strong pressure from New York, Van Buren's home state, in favor of the tariff, and argues that the Little Magician thought a tariff that passed might be even more useful to the Jacksonians than one that failed. In either case, the effect on Southern politicians was the same; they were badly beaten and believed that Van Buren and the Jacksonians had betrayed them. For a fuller version of this approach, see Remini, "Martin Van Buren and the Tariff of Abominations."

52. Wiltse, *Calhoun*, 1:368.

53. *Ibid.*, p. 369.

54. Stanwood, *American Tariff Controversies*, 1:273.

55. *Ibid.*, 1:289–90; Wiltse, *Calhoun*, 1:370.

56. Stanwood, *American Tariff Controversies*, 1:259; Wiltse, *Calhoun*, 1:371–72.

57. Wiltse, *Calhoun*, 1:380.

58. *Ibid.*, 1:372–73; Freehling, *Prelude to Civil War*, pp. 147–48.

59. Freehling, *Prelude to Civil War*, pp. 148–49.

60. Wiltse, *Calhoun*, 1:378.

61. The "Exposition" can be found in Calhoun, *Works*, ed. by Crallé, 6:1–59. This is Calhoun's original text, and does not include the changes made by the South Carolina legislature before the essay was printed.

62. *Ibid.*, p. 12.

63. Quoted in Van Deusen, *Jacksonian Era*, p. 39.

64. Coit, *Calhoun*, p. 492; Nevins, *Ordeal of the Union*, 1:281.

65. Coit, *Calhoun*, p. 188.

66. Calhoun, *Works*, 6:25–26.

67. *Ibid.*, pp. 29–30.

68. *Ibid.*, pp. 50–51.

69. *Ibid.*, p. 51.
70. Freehling, *Prelude to Civil War*, p. 146.
71. Calhoun, *Works*, 6:49.
72. *Ibid.*, p. 59.
73. Moore, *Social Origins of Dictatorship and Democracy*, p. 114.
74. Coit, *Calhoun*, p. 166.
75. Moore, *Social Origins of Dictatorship and Democracy*, p. 152.
76. Freehling, *Prelude to Civil War*, pp. 175–76.
77. Wiltse, *Calhoun*, 2:55.
78. *Ibid.*, p. 57.
79. *Ibid.*, p. 60.
80. Freehling, *Prelude to Civil War*, p. 186.
81. *Ibid.*, p. 131.
82. Freehling, ed., *Nullification Era*, pp. 118, 118–19.
83. *Ibid.*, pp. 137–38.
84. Wiltse, *Calhoun*, 2:115.
85. *Ibid.*, 2:124.
86. *Ibid.*, 2:125.
87. *Worchester v. Georgia*, 6 Peters 512–559 (1832).
88. Freehling, *Prelude to Civil War*, pp. 232–33.
89. *Ibid.*, p. 257.
90. Wiltse, *Calhoun*, 2:144.
91. *Ibid.*, 2:145.
92. Freehling, *Prelude to Civil War*, p. 262.
93. Freehling, ed., *Nullification Era*, p. 152.
94. Freehling, *Prelude to Civil War*, p. 265.
95. Stanwood, *American Tariff Controversies*, 1:388–90; Wiltse, *Calhoun*, 2:170.
96. Wiltse, *Calhoun*, 2:171.
97. Freehling, ed., *Nullification Era*, pp. 155–56, 159, 163 (italics in the original).
98. Wiltse, *Calhoun*, 2:172.
99. Coit, *Calhoun*, p. 253.
100. Wiltse, *Calhoun*, 2:177.

5 / PATTERNS OF POLITICS

1. Key, "Theory of Critical Elections."
2. Lowi, "American Business, Public Policy," pp. 689–90.
3. *Ibid.*, p. 690.
4. Schattschneider, *Politics, Pressures, and the Tariff.*
5. Lowi, "Party, Policy, and Constitution," p. 255.
6. Lowi, "Four Systems," p. 310 (fn).
7. Greenberg et al., "Developing Public Policy Theory."
8. Lowi, "Four Systems," and "Decision Making vs. Policy Making."
9. Lowi, "Four Systems," p. 299 (his italics).
10. See, for example, Corwin, *President*, or Koenig, *Chief Executive.*
11. Robinson, "Crisis," p. 510.
12. *New York Times*, Dec. 9, 1972, p. 1.
13. For a short survey, see Bracher, "Crisis Government."
14. *Ibid.*, p. 515, gives a partial listing.
15. See Kesselman, "Order or Movement?" for a useful discussion on this point.

16. Grew, "Crises of Political Development," p. 2.

17. Flanagan and Mundt, "Comparative Analysis of Historical Case Studies," p. 2.

18. Easton, *Systems Analysis of Political Life.*

19. Leites, *On the Games of Politics in France,* esp. pp. 148–68.

20. Eckstein, "Authority Patterns," pp. 1148–49.

21. Edelman, *Symbolic Uses of Politics,* esp. ch. 2.

22. For a description of such subsystems, see Freeman, *Political Process.*

23. Truman, *Governmental Process,* pp. 510–24.

24. Simon, *Administrative Behavior,* pp. 126–27.

25. The idea of a presidential "contingency system" is developed by James S. Young in his work in progress on the presidency. His study, *Washington Community,* clearly shows the absence of any such settled system during the War of 1812.

6 / POLITICAL CHANGE IN THE UNITED STATES

1. Greenberg, et al., "Developing Public Policy Theory."

2. Eckstein, "Case Studies and Theory in Political Science," p. 85.

3. Greenberg et al., "Developing Public Policy Theory," pp. 10–12.

4. Eckstein, "Case Studies and Theory in Political Science," p. 93.

5. Tilly, ed., *Formation of National States,* pp. 6, 21.

6. Flanagan and Mundt, "Comparative Analysis of Historical Case Studies," p. 2.

7. Almond, Flanagan, and Mundt, *Crisis, Choice, and Change.*

8. Finch and Forsythe, "Theories of American Political Change," pp. 55–71.

9. Huntington, "The Change to Change," p. 315.

10. Like several paragraphs in this chapter, Figure 6.1 is based on Finch and Forsythe, "Theories of American Political Change." I am very grateful to Gerald Finch for permission to use in this essay these products of our joint work.

11. Easton, *Systems Analysis of Political Life.*

12. Edelman, *Politics as Symbolic Action,* pp. 3–4.

13. Almond, Flanagan, and Mundt, *Crisis, Choice, and Change,* p. 12.

14. Tilly, ed., *Formation of National States,* p. 620.

15. Burnham, *Critical Elections,* p. 135.

16. Ash, *Social Movements in America,* p. 11.

17. Piven and Cloward, *Regulating the Poor,* p. 7.

18. See, for example, Finch, "Physical Change and Partisan Change."

19. Mansfield, "Dispersion of Authority in Congress"; Price, "Congressional Career"; Polsby, "Institutionalization of the House of Representatives."

20. Cronin, *State of the Presidency,* ch. 5.

21. Fisher, *President and Congress;* Funston, "The Supreme Court and Critical Elections."

22. Michels, *Political Parties;* Allison, *Essence of Decision,* ch. 5.

23. Young, *Washington Community.*

24. O'Connor, *Fiscal Crisis of the State,* ch. 4.

25. Ilchman and Uphoff, *Political Economy of Change,* pp. 201–2.

26. Moore, *Social Origins of Dictatorship and Democracy,* p. 470.

27. Edelman, *Symbolic Uses of Politics,* esp. ch. 2.

28. Etzioni, *Complex Organizations,* makes similar distinctions, pp. 5–6.

29. Scott, *Comparative Political Corruption,* p. 108 and *passim.*

30. Gerth and Mills, eds., *From Max Weber,* p. 79.

31. O'Connor, *Fiscal Crisis of the State,* ch. 6.

32. Edelman, *Symbolic Uses of Politics.*

33. Katznelson and Kesselman, "Repression or Legitimacy?" p. 9.

34. Piven and Cloward, *Regulating the Poor.*

35. See Gerth and Mills, eds., *From Max Weber*, pp. 78–79, for a short exposition. For a fuller treatment, see Weber, *Theory of Social and Economic Organization*, Part III, pp. 324–92.

36. Zolberg, *Creating Political Order*, p. 137.

37. Lipset, *First New Nation*, ch. 1.

38. Gerth and Mills, eds., *From Max Weber*, p. 184.

39. See *Long Term Economic Growth.*

40. Levy, "A 150-Year Study of Political Violence in the U.S."

41. Funston, "The Supreme Court and Critical Elections."

42. Burnham, *Critical Elections*, p. 10 (fn.).

43. Funston, "The Supreme Court and Critical Elections"; Ginsberg, "Elections and Public Policy."

44. Finch and Forsythe, "Theories of American Political Change."

45. Ginsberg, "Elections and Public Policy."

/ BIBLIOGRAPHY

Adams, Henry Carter. *Taxation in the United States, 1789–1816.* Baltimore: Johns Hopkins University Press, 1884.

Allison, Graham. *Essence of Decision.* Boston: Little, Brown, 1971.

Almond, Gabriel, Scott C. Flanagan, and Robert J. Mundt, eds. *Crisis, Choice, and Change.* Boston: Little, Brown, 1973.

American State Papers: Finance. Washington: Gales and Seaton, 1832–1861.

Ash, Roberta T. *Social Movements in America.* Chicago: Rand McNally, 1972.

Baldwin, Leland D. *Whiskey Rebels: The Story of a Frontier Uprising.* Pittsburgh: University of Pittsburgh Press, 1939.

Balinky, Alexander. *Albert Gallatin: Fiscal Theories and Policies.* New Brunswick, N.J.: Rutgers University Press, 1958.

Barnard, Chester A. *The Functions of the Executive.* Cambridge: Harvard University Press, 1968.

Beard, Charles A. *An Economic Interpretation of the United States Constitution.* New York: Macmillan, 1956.

—— *Economic Origins of Jeffersonian Democracy.* New York: Macmillan, 1943.

Bracher, Karl D. "Crisis Government," *International Encyclopedia of the Social Sciences,* 3:514–18. New York: Macmillan, 1968.

Brown, Robert H. *The Republic in Peril: 1812.* New York: Norton, 1971.

Bruchey, Stuart. *The Roots of American Economic Growth: 1607–1861.* New York: Harper and Row, 1965.

Burnham, Walter Dean. *Critical Elections and the Mainsprings of American Politics.* New York: Norton, 1970.

Budget of the United States Government, Fiscal Year 1977. Washington: Government Printing Office, 1976.

Calhoun, John C. *Works*, Richard K. Crallé, ed. Vol. 6. New York: Russell and Russell, 1968.

Chambers, William N. *Political Parties in the New Nation.* New York: Oxford University Press, 1963.

Coit, Margaret L. *John C. Calhoun: American Portrait.* Boston: Houghton Mifflin, 1950.

Corwin, Edward S. *The President: Office and Powers.* 4th rev. ed. New York: New York University Press, 1957.

Cronin, Thomas E. *The State of the Presidency.* Boston: Little, Brown, 1975.

Current, Richard N. *Daniel Webster and the Rise of National Conservatism.* Boston: Little, Brown, 1955.

Dangerfield, George. *The Awakening of American Nationalism, 1815–1828.* New York: Harper and Row, 1965.

Dauer, Manning. *The Adams Federalists.* Baltimore: Johns Hopkins University Press, 1953.

Davis, W. W. H. *The Fries Rebellion: 1798–1799.* Doylestown, Pa.: Douglastown Publishing, 1899.

Dickerson, Oliver M. *The Navigation Acts and the American Revolution.* New York: A. S. Barnes, 1963.

Easton, David. *A Systems Analysis of Political Life.* New York: Wiley, 1965.

Eckstein, Harry. "Authority Patterns: A Structural Basis for Political Inquiry," *American Political Science Review* 67 (1973):1142–61.

—— "Case Study and Theory in Political Science," in *Handbook of Political Science,* Fred I. Greenstein and Nelson W. Polsby, eds., 7:79–139. Reading, Mass.: Addison-Wesley, 1975.

Edelman, Murray. *Politics as Symbolic Action.* Chicago: Markham, 1971.

—— *The Symbolic Uses of Politics.* Urbana, Ill.: University of Illinois Press, 1964.

Elton, G. R. *The Tudor Constitution.* London: Cambridge University Press, 1965.

Etzioni, Amatai. *A Comprehensive Analysis of Complex Organizations.* New York: Free Press, 1961.

Farrand, Max, ed. *The Records of the Federal Convention of 1781,* vol. 1. New Haven: Yale University Press, 1966.

Federalist Papers. New York: New American Library, 1961.

Ferguson, E. James. *The Power of the Purse: A History of American Public Finance, 1776–1790.* Chapel Hill: University of North Carolina Press, 1961.

Finch, Gerald B. "Physical Change and Partisan Change: The Emergence of a New American Electorate, 1952–1972," in *The Future of Political Parties: Sage Electoral Studies Yearbook,* Louis Maisel and Paul M. Sacks, eds., 1 (1975): 13–62.

Finch, Gerald B. and Dall W. Forsythe. "Theories of American Political Change." Mimeo: prepared for delivery at the Annual Meeting of the American Political Science Association, 1976.

Fish, Carl Russell. *The Civil Service and Patronage.* New York: Russell and Russell, 1963.

Fisher, Louis. *President and Congress.* New York: Free Press, 1972.

Flanagan, Scott C. and Robert J. Mundt. "Comparative Analysis of Historical Case Studies: Crisis, Choice, and Change." Mimeo: prepared for delivery at the Annual Meeting of the American Political Science Association, 1972.

Freehling, William W. *Prelude to Civil War: The Nullification Controversy in South Carolina, 1816–1836.* New York: Harper and Row, 1965.

Freehling, William W., ed. *The Nullification Era: A Documentary Record.* New York: Harper and Row, 1967.

Freeman, J. Leiper. *The Political Process.* Rev. ed. New York: Random House, 1966.

Funston, Richard. "The Supreme Court and Critical Elections," *American Political Science Review* 69 (1975):795–811.

Gerth, H. H. and C. W. Mills, eds. *From Max Weber: Essays in Sociology.* New York: Oxford University Press, 1958.

Ginsberg, Benjamin. "Elections and Public Policy," *American Political Science Review* 70 (1976):41–49.

Greenberg, George, Jeffrey A. Miller, Lawrence B. Mohr, and Bruce C. Vladek. "Developing Public Policy Theory: Perspectives from Empirical Research." Mimeo: Institute of Public Policy Studies Discussion Paper #81, 1975.

Greenstone, J. David and Paul E. Peterson. *Race and Authority in Urban Politics.* New York: Russell Sage Foundation, 1973.

Grew, Raymond. "Crises of Political Development." Mimeo: prepared for delivery at the Annual Meeting of the American Political Science Association, 1972.

Hartz, Louis. *The Liberal Tradition in America.* New York: Harcourt, Brace, and World, 1955.

Historical Statistics of the United States: Colonial Times to 1957. Washington: Government Printing Office, 1960.

Huntington, Samuel P. "The Change to Change: Modernization and Development and Politics," *Comparative Politics* 3 (1971):283–322.

—— *Political Order in Changing Societies.* New Haven: Yale University Press, 1968.

Ilchman, Warren F. and Norman T. Uphoff. *The Political Economy of Change.* Berkeley: University of California Press, 1971.

Jensen, Merrill. *The New Nation.* New York: Vintage, 1950.

Johnson's Dictionary: A Modern Selection, E. L. McAdam Jr. and George Milne, eds. New York: Pantheon, 1963.

Katznelson, Ira and Mark Kesselman. "Repression or Legitimacy? Choices in the Language of Social Research." Mimeo: no date.

Kesselman, Mark. "Order or Movement: The Literature of Political Development as Ideology," *World Politics* 26 (1973):139–54.

Key, V. O. "A Theory of Critical Elections," *Journal of Politics* 17 (1955):3–18.

Koenig, Louis W. *The Chief Executive.* New York: Harcourt, Brace and World, 1964.

Kurtz, Stephen G. *The Presidency of John Adams.* Philadelphia: University of Pennsylvania Press, 1957.

Leites, Nathan C. *On the Game of Politics in France.* Stanford: Stanford University Press, 1959.

Levy, Sheldon G. "A 150-Year Study of Political Violence in the United States," in *Violence in America,* Hugh Graham Davis and Ted Robert Gurr, eds. New York: Signet, 1969.

Lipset, Semour Martin. *The First New Nation.* New York: Basic Books, 1963.

Longterm Economic Growth, 1860–1970, Washington: Government Printing Office, 1973.

Lowi, Theodore J. "American Business, Public Policy, Case Studies, and Political Theory," *World Politics* 16 (1964):677–715.

—— *American Government: Incomplete Conquest.* Hinsdale, Ill.: Dryden Press, 1976.

—— "Decision Making vs. Policy Making: Towards an Antidote for Technocracy," *Public Administration Review* 30 (1970):314–25.

—— "Four Systems of Policy, Politics, and Choice," *Public Administration Review* 33 (1972):298–310.

—— "Party, Policy, and Constitution in America," in *The American Party Systems: Stages of Political Development,* W. N. Chambers and W. D. Burnham, eds. New York: Oxford University Press, 1967.

MacRae, Duncan and James A. Meldrum. "Critical Elections in Illinois: 1888–1958," *American Political Science Review* 54 (1960):669–83.

Malone, Dumas. *Jefferson and His Times.* 4 vols. Boston: Little, Brown, 1951–1970.

Mansfield, Harvey D., Sr. "The Dispersion of Authority in Congress," in *Congress Against the President: Proceedings of the Academy of Political Science* 32 (1975):1–19.

Merritt, Richard L. *Symbols of American Community, 1735–1775.* New Haven: Yale University Press, 1966.

Michels, Robert. *Political Parties.* Glencoe Mills, Ill.: Free Press, 1949.

Miller, John C. *Alexander Hamilton: Portrait in Paradox.* New York: Harper and Row, 1959.

—— *The Federalist Era, 1789–1801.* New York: Harper and Row, 1960.

—— *Origins of the American Revolution.* Boston: Little, Brown, 1943.

Mitchell, Broadus. *Alexander Hamilton.* 2 vols. New York: Macmillan, 1957–62.

Moore, Barrington. *Social Origins of Dictatorship and Democracy.* Boston: Beacon, 1966.

Morgan, Edmund S. *The Birth of the Republic, 1763–1789.* Chicago: University of Chicago Press, 1956.

Morris, Richard B., ed. *Alexander Hamilton and the Founding of the Nation.* New York: Harper and Row, 1969.

Mosca, Gaetano. *The Ruling Class.* New York: McGraw, Hill, 1939.

Nevins, Allan. *The Ordeal of the Nation*. Vol. 1. New York: Scribners, 1947.

New York Times, 1972.

O'Connor, James. *The Fiscal Crisis of the State*. New York: St. Martins, 1973.

Piven, Frances Fox and Richard A. Cloward. *Regulating the Poor: The Functions of Public Relief*. New York: Random House, 1971.

Polsby, Nelson W. "The Institutionalization of the House of Representatives," *American Political Science Review* 62 (1968):144–68.

Price, H. Douglas. "The Congressional Career: Then and Now," in *Congressional Behavior*, Nelson W. Polsby, ed. New York: Random House, 1972.

Pye, Lucian W. and Sidney Verba, eds. *Political Culture and Political Development*. Princeton: Princeton University Press, 1965.

Remini, Robert V. "Martin Van Buren and the Tariff of Abominations," *American Historical Review* 63 (1958):903–17.

The Reports of Alexander Hamilton, Jacob E. Cooke, ed. New York: Harper and Row, 1964.

Robinson, James A. "Crisis," in *International Encyclopedia of the Social Sciences*, 3:510–14. New York: Macmillan, 1968.

Rossiter, Clinton. *Alexander Hamilton and the Constitution*. New York: Harcourt, Brace and World, 1964.

Schattschneider, E. E. *Politics, Pressures, and the Tariff*. New York: Prentice-Hall, 1935.

Scott, James C. *Comparative Political Corruption*. Englewood Cliffs, N.J.: Prentice-Hall, 1972.

Simon, Herbert. *Administrative Behavior*. New York: Free Press, 1965.

Singer, J. David. *A General Systems Taxonomy for Political Science*. New York: General Learning Press, 1971.

Smelser, Marshall. *The Democratic Republic, 1801–1815*. New York: Harper and Row, 1968.

Smith, Page. "David Ramsay and the Causes of the American Revolution," *William and Mary Quarterly* 17 (1960):51–77.

Stanwood, Edward. *American Tariff Controversies in the Nineteenth Century*. 2 vols. New York: Russell and Russell, 1967.

Statistical Abstract of the United States. Washington: Government Printing Office, 1975.

Sydnor, Charles S. *The Development of Southern Sectionalism, 1818–1848*. Baton Rouge, La.: Louisiana State University Press, 1948.

Taussig, F. W. *The Tariff History of the United States*. 8th rev. ed. New York: Putnam, 1931.

Tilly, Charles, ed. *The Formation of National States in Western Europe*. Princeton: Princeton University Press, 1975.

Truman, David B. *The Governmental Process*. New York: Knopf, 1951.

Van Deusen, Glyndon G. *The Jacksonian Era*. New York: Harper and Row, 1959.

Walters, Raymond, Jr. *Albert Gallatin: Jeffersonian Financier and Diplomat*. New York: Macmillan, 1957.

Weber, Max. *The Theory of Social and Economic Organization*. New York: Oxford University Press, 1947.

White, Leonard D. *The Federalists*. New York: Macmillan, 1948.

—— *The Jeffersonians*. New York: Macmillan, 1951.

Williams, E. Neville. *The Eighteenth-Century Constitution*. London: Cambridge University Press, 1960.

Wiltse, Charles M. *John C. Calhoun*. 2 vols. New York: Russell and Russell, 1970.

Woodbury, Margaret. *Public Opinion in Philadelphia, 1789–1801*. Northampton, Mass.: Smith College, 1919.

Wright, Esmond. *Fabric of Freedom, 1763–1780*. New York: Hill and Wang, 1961.

Young, James S. *The Washington Community, 1800–1828*. New York: Columbia University Press, 1966.

Zolberg, Aristide. *Creating Political Order: The Party States of West Africa*. Chicago: Rand McNally, 1966.

/ INDEX